Acknowledgements

We would like to thank the following people: Professor Ann Buchanan, St Hilda's College, University of Oxford; Professor Charles Desforges OBE, University of Exeter; Geoff Hannan, educationalist, writer and broadcaster; Professor David Hargreaves, Wolfson College, University of Cambridge; Professor Steve Higgins, Durham University; David Hyner, Stretch Development; Bill Morris, director of the Education Improvement Partnership, Leicester; Professor Steve Strand, University of Oxford; and Gary Wilson, freelance consultant.

CONTENTS

Let others lead small lives, but not you.
Let others argue over small things, but
not you. Let others cry over small hurts,
but not you. Let others leave their future
in someone else's hands, but not you.

Jim Rohn

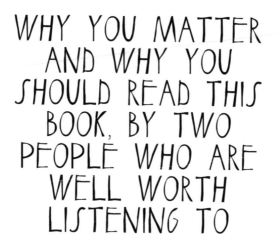

WHY YOU MATTER AND WHY YOU SHOULD READ THIS BOOK, BY TWO PEOPLE WHO ARE WELL WORTH LISTENING TO

Foreword by
Shonette Bason-Wood

I'm old enough now (eek!) to remember a time before we had fabulous teaching assistants and brilliant classroom assistants. They were the bad old days when the teacher was expected to do everything in classrooms full to the brim.

I will always remember the first time I ever had a classroom assistant. I wasn't alone any more – hooray! A head chef can't function without the sous chef – and it's the same in the modern

classroom. We simply need properly trained, totally brilliant classroom and teaching assistants to share the ever increasing load.

Working with children demands dedication, commitment and superhero powers. Adults who turn up every day of the school year and work with the interests of the children first and foremost in their minds are, to me, truly brilliant. At the drop of a hat, a superb classroom assistant might cover another staff member's absence, take an extra playground or dinner duty and still help out at the disco on a school night. Phew!

In my opinion, teaching assistants are the most undervalued resource in education. Ask any teacher if they would rather have an interactive

whiteboard or another adult to support them, and I bet every single one would opt for the fellow human being.

The job is exhausting. Very often there isn't a moment in the school day for a cuppa (or a wee!), and sometimes people forget to say thank you. This book is designed to inspire and invigorate you, but most of all it's a reminder of how crucial you are. *You* impact on individual pupil learning, and the classroom climate and help to reduce teacher stress. *You* make a real difference – in fact, *you* are a life changer. Thank you.

(Shonette is an early years teacher and internationally renowned speaker. Her work is showcased at www. shonettebasonwood.com.)

Foreword by David Taylor

When Andy asked me to write this foreword, I said yes without hesitation.

And then I hesitated.

Three challenges came to mind – a lack of time, talent and education – and, on that last point alone, who am I to write the foreword to a book for classroom assistants, often the unsung heroes in our schools, society and communities,

who work tirelessly alongside our wonderful teachers to help young people fulfil their potential?

Then I thought, 'well, who actually bothers to read the forewords in books?' So, if these words ever actually get published, I urge you to skip them – after all, Andy, Chris and Gary are such brilliant storytellers, share so many practical how-tos and have that rare gift of making each and every reader feel the book has been written just for them – you'll want to get on with reading the book.

And more – this truly unique book is so much more than its title – it is a guide, a bible – that when applied will transform our education system – academic and beyond – because it inspires, empowers and gives permission to all who read it, to unlock and unleash the strengths, talents and passions in themselves, and in everyone else. This book deserves to be in every classroom, in every school in the world.

Andy is very kind about my books, saying that *The Naked Leader Experience* changed his life. Thank you, Andy. With this book, you, Gary and Chris will change lives every single day, every single hour and in every single second.

(David Taylor is an internationally renowned author, speaker and Prince's Trust guru. His work is showcased at www. nakedleader.com.)

AN OPENING
THOUGHT

As a society we have fallen prey to what Larry Dossey calls 'time-sickness' – the belief that 'time is getting away … and that you must pedal faster and faster to keep up'.[1] On this speeding treadmill, we have become hungry for information and fearful of missing out – beautifully text-languaged as 'FOMO'. As we skim and graze, picking up one piece of entertaining information before moving on to the next in hasty bursts, we have become addicted to trivia.

---

1   Larry Dossey, *Space, Time and Medicine* (Boston, MA: Shambhala Publications, 1982), pp. 50–51.

We've learned to do this. As Sir Ken Robinson acknowledges, if you're over the age of 25, technology is your second language, something you've picked up as you've gone along. For today's children, however, technology is their first language.[2] They are totally fluent in 'iPad' and 'Xbox'. Information is openly accessible and speed is the new intelligence.

Thinking aloud, we wonder whether children may lose the ability to seek the stillness that connects them to who they are, and instead find themselves engulfed in boredom and/or loneliness. We wonder whether the constant churn of trivia and their addiction to superficial information will keep young people from attending to relationships. Might the impatience and anxiety that speed entails diminish their gratitude and empathy? Will their desire to know about everything result in them knowing nothing? These are huge questions and, in our lifetimes, we may never get to know the answers.

Social science suggests that our brains did not evolve to operate instinctively in today's complex world. Humans are resilient and we will adapt. But the world is moving faster than our brains can adapt so we are playing catch-up. Speed frees up time but, ask yourself, what do

---

2   Ken Robinson, Bring On the Learning Revolution! *TED.com* (May 2010). Transcript available at: https://www.ted.com/talks/sir_ken_robinson_bring_on_the_revolution/transcript?language=en.

you do with that extra time? There's a strong likelihood that you invest that saved time in more fast stuff. Is that wise? We are living life fast but are we living it well?

This book is partly about your profession but it is entirely about *you*. The lessons of engagement, positivity and relationships are not just for the classroom, they extend across all domains of your life.

We're hoping that you might therefore consider slowing down, just a tad. Because thinking time, and in particular stillness, is an increasingly rare commodity. There's a likelihood that you will feel compelled to race through this book, impatiently skimming for useful nuggets. If this is the case, you will have neither the time nor the mental space to make proper sense of the information or sustain it through deeper thought.

Our plea is to chew on it rather than swallow it whole.

Bon appétit!

BRILLIANT
CLASSROOM
ASSISTANT

REGISTRATION

Now, you can't accuse us of skimming the surface for this book. We've consulted far and wide, even to the extent of unearthing pearls from the Wiki-goldmine of everything. So here's a stunning fact: the Catholic Church has appointed a patron saint for just about everything (even parts of your body!). Here are a few of our faves: St Fiacre is the patron saint of haemorrhoids, Thomas of Green is the patron saint of 'sensitive knees' and, in a moment of marketing enlightenment, Aspren is the patron saint of headaches. Yes, really (does Wikipedia ever lie?). Simon of Trent is the patron saint of kidnap victims. Somewhat deliciously, there is also a patron saint of failures, Birgitta of Sweden, who presumably failed to impress Ofsted on more than one occasion.

The salient point of all these shenanigans is that most occupations have been given a patron. So, for example, St Elmo is supposed to look over all those who work at great heights and Anthony the Abbot is the guardian of gravediggers. Teachers are greedy – they have two: John Baptist de la Salle and St Catherine. There is literally an A (Adrian of Nicomedia, saint of arms dealers) to Z (Zita, saint of domestic servants) of dead saints, each allocated to an occupation.

If you scour the list you'll find that every occupation has a nominated guardian whom those who decide such things deem fit and proper enough to be looking after their well-being. That is, except one. So who is it that either doesn't need looking after or is not worthy of being bestowed with a patron? Classroom assistants, that's who. So, if there's nobody 'up there' cheering you on, you might need to find the resources within yourself.

Before the off, a very quick word about style and substance. If you are expecting a learned tome full of academia with a considered critique of the effectiveness of government policy since 1870, this is not the book for you. But if you want a book that is easy to read on the sun-kissed deckchairs of Skegness during your well-earned summer holidays, or a book you can dip into for a quick dose of inspiration and some nifty ideas you could use in the classroom tomorrow, you are probably in the right zone.

We are big believers in what we call 'the magpie technique'. Magpies are birds which steal from other birds' nests. In education, by and large, teachers and other classroom assistants are not too precious about their ideas – it is an open forum in which there is a natural exchange of expertise. We learn by watching others and discussing ideas with them. If someone else is getting stellar results, then why not have a peek

at what they're doing and make it work for you? That's what we've done, so this book represents some of the best ideas and techniques we've come across on our travels. We will occasionally throw in a quote, anecdote or big thought that needs highlighting and, in retro-style, we've brought thinking back *inside* the box. Oh, and there's a whole load of top tips too.

So buckle up and safety goggles on – here's our guide to being brilliant. Our job is to make you smile, make you think and make you want to be the very best classroom assistant you can possibly be.

We're proud to have you aboard.

Lesson 1

JOB, CAREER
OR CALLING?

Hell, there are no rules here – we're trying to accomplish something.

Thomas Edison

Chris and Gary have a combined seventy years of teaching experience or, put differently, they have clocked up 50,000 lessons between them. And then there's our writing buddy, Andy – 'Dr of Happiness' no less – who has 400 school visits under his belt, some of which have been in far off lands. Now, we could wax lyrical about the highs and lows of our kaleidoscope of lessons, in which we have taught subjects as

diverse as design technology and French, literacy and drama to kids from primary through to A level, but that is not the purpose of this book.

Put simply, we've had a ball. It has been a joy to be able to wake up every morning and look forward to going to work, rubbing shoulders with some amazing people along the way. The vast majority of the children have been fantastic. Talk about a kaleidoscope; there couldn't have been a more colourful or diverse bunch. We've loved them all – yes, even the most challenging ones. How we wish we had made a note through the years of all the characters we've met. Then there are the staff: yes, we use the term 'staff' deliberately because a school is about far more than just the teachers. A successful school has a team of incredibly dedicated people at every level. Teachers cannot possibly weave their web of magic without the contribution of the estate management staff, the admin team, reception staff, lunchtime supervisors, IT technicians and the head teacher.

Awesome schools are a thriving community with brilliant staff in all these roles. But there's one area that we feel is especially important – a cog without which the wheels on the school fail to go round and round. A team who have such a tough role but who can make such a massive difference to the learning and well-being of the children. What's more, these individuals can also add sparkle to the classroom and can help breathe health and vitality into the teachers around them. Yet, despite their potentially life changing importance, this is a group which is often undervalued, underpaid and underappreciated. As you have already learned, they don't even have a patron saint.

Our task in this book is to share our enthusiasm, as well as our zeal and zest, with those of you who are the unsung heroes of modern day education: the humble classroom assistants. And we say 'humble' deliberately, because you generally are. Let's lay our cards on the table at the outset: there's a big fat chance that you are undervalued by the school community. Plus, there's also a fair-to-middling probability that you are underestimating your own importance. The role of the classroom assistant has been massively downplayed, so we want to raise your knowledge and confidence towards the upper echelons of 'world class'. We want to get you *excited* about being a classroom assistant.

7

·BEST· place in the world!

You have probably already cottoned on to the idea that we believe that schools are among the best places in the world, and that working in a school is truly magical. However, the days are long and there's no doubt that your job can be physically and emotionally exhausting. We won't pretend otherwise. We sometimes liken the job of teaching kids to one of those super hand dryers you come across in smart hotels – you know, the ones which almost drag your fingernails out of your finger ends with the powerful rush of air. You have to look away because everything's flapping. There is a huge expenditure of energy. Whether you are a teacher or a brilliant classroom assistant, you will go home at the end of the day feeling drained. But there's 'good' and 'bad' exhaustion. Bad exhaustion is

when you get home having lost a few battles, slump wearily into a chair and wonder why you bothered becoming a classroom assistant at all. Good exhaustion is to slump into your chair with a cuppa and a wry smile on your face because you've made a difference.

This feeling of genuinely making a difference is a really big deal. In the hurly-burly of the modern school, classroom assistants can sometimes simply forget the power of their influence. So this book is a cold flannel in the face of a reminder. The chances are that you are not in it for the money because, let's face it, there are quicker ways to get rich. But if we expand the concept of 'rich' away from your bank balance and towards wealth in the widest sense of the term, the feeling of making a difference is a massive credit to your happiness account.

We want you to puff out your chest with pride, as well as defend the profession that all too often outsiders attempt to denigrate. It was our recent good fortune to take a taxi in London on our way to a conference where we were to be keynote speakers. Now, you may think that riding in a black cab is not necessarily right up there in terms of the thrills and spills of life, but

as a couple of teachers from Leicester, Chris and Gary got a bit excited. The cabbie was one of those affable guys who likes to engage with his passengers. He enquired as to what had brought us down to the great metropolis, so we explained that we were teachers.

Those of us who work in education know that in any social setting, the mere mention of schools or teaching is an open invitation to whoever we are with to share their thoughts on education. After all, we're all experts – we all went to school, didn't we? So, the floodgates of conversation opened and we were treated to his own personal diatribe on schools and kids today. His perception was pretty much fed by the usual media stereotypes: things aren't as good as they used to be, they aren't as good as they could be, young people are running riot and other countries do it much better than we do. It seems to us that, over all our years of experience, the same narrative seems to have informed pretty much every secretary of state for education as well.

Forgive us for being a bit tetchy on the subject, but it is our natural instinct to ask when *exactly* was this golden age of education when everything was so much more rosy? Can someone please tell us when were these heady days of no one misbehaving in class and everyone leaving with a Shakespearean grasp of English

literature and a Newtonian understanding of the laws of physics? Forsooth, don't believe the propaganda. Young people were challenging us thirty years ago, they are still testing us now and they will continue to push the boundaries of authority in thirty years' time. That's what young people do.

Society seems to have morphed such that the modern family resembles a cohort of blue-arsed flies, buzzing around like crazy. As life has speeded up, so jobs have changed and technology has muscled its way to centre stage, which has in turn affected norms of behaviour. Today's generation of children are pushing different boundaries to those of the generations before them. We find that some school staff agree with the taxi driver that schools were better back in the day. Whatever the rights and wrongs of that argument, our point is that those days are gone.

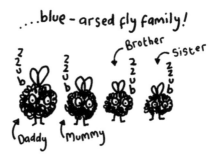

...blue - arsed fly family!

Whether 'change' is good or bad is a moot point. We are here, now, and we have to deal with the education system and society as it really is, not how we'd like it to be. If the challenges of education have moved on then so must our thinking and techniques. So, the focus of this book is not only about changing the education system but also tweaking ourselves. And speaking of change, we've noticed that the standard of all of the school staff we work with is becoming better and better. And this is what really matters.

The national discourse about education has operated at many different levels over the last fifty years or so. We have expended shed loads of energy on discussing the structures of schooling at secondary level. Would it be more advantageous to have grammar schools, comprehensive schools, grant maintained schools, free schools, academies …? The list goes on. As a country we have invested mega millions in buildings in the belief that shiny new glass and steel schools will provide a better learning environment. We have seen wagon trains of gleaming new curriculum and assessment bandwagons roll into town and then, in due course, roll out again. But it can be difficult to demonstrate empirically that any of this has made a difference.

We don't think we can make it any clearer than this: donning our 'good old days' rose-tinted spectacles does us no favours at all. Those days, if they ever existed at all, are long gone. Continuing to hang on to them will stop us fully functioning in the present. So, rather than argue about whether the current system is good or bad, let's stick with an age-old truth: once the lesson has started the name of the game has not changed. It is the quality of that interaction between the children and those leading the learning which determines how good the outcomes will be.

Meanwhile, back in the taxi, we are due to be on the conference platform in about twenty-five minutes. Traffic around Trafalgar Square is almost stationary and yet, despite him knowing the London streets like the proverbial back of his hand, we sit stalled in the traffic, defending our profession. Interestingly, although we were bursting to tell him that the standard of taxi driving has declined in the last ten years, and that last time we were here our taxi driver took a short cut and was incredibly polite, we resisted. It would have been rude and we are professionals after all.

As we sat in the traffic jam we had time to reflect on our time in education and agreed that one of the biggest innovations in the last ten years has been the arrival in schools of classroom

assistants. And *hurrah*, what a refreshing revolution it's been. At the outset of our illustrious careers there was no such thing – classroom assistants literally had not been invented. There was one teacher and a mass of kids (gulp). It was sink or swim. But classroom assistants are here, and are here to stay, so this book has been designed to help all of those who carry out this vital role to be not just ordinary professionals on the periphery of the learning process, but central players in creating a world class learning environment.

We use the term 'classroom assistant' to cover a wide range of specific titles that are never ending and ever changing. However, they all have a role in the classroom which is different to that of the teacher, and it is that function we explore in the following pages.

The best and most brilliant classroom assistants make a huge difference to the children's learning, so the task in this book has been to unpick all the threads in the tapestry to enrich and inspire all those who aspire to be the very best version of themselves they can possibly be. You might be baulking at the fact that we have set our sights so high. 'Brilliant' is not for the faint-hearted and, let's face it, it's a whole lot easier to be mediocre. But we reason that there wouldn't be much point in expending all our energy in writing a book called 'The Art of Being a

Bog-Standard Classroom Assistant'. If we're going to embark on this journey together, let's be big and bold and aim for the very top – because if we don't do that, we would be letting the children and ourselves down.

Wouldn't be much point in this

THE ART OF BEING A
BOG-STANDARD
CLASSROOM
ASSISTANT

If you asked a standard person on the Clapham omnibus what a classroom assistant does, you would probably get an answer along the lines of 'providing an extra pair of hands' in the classroom. In the early days this just about covered it and, in so far as he knew anything about it, it is as near as our London taxi driver would have got. We have often described the business of education as being like a thousand piece jigsaw, and the challenge for each and every one of us is to assemble as many of those pieces as possible at any one point in time. Likewise, the role of classroom assistant is not one which carries an easy one-size-fits-all description. It is a

multifaceted job so coming up with a precise definition is like trying to locate subatomic particles. What the role embodies, however, is crucial.

Around ten years ago, a very well-connected government adviser spoke at a conference we attended. He blasted schools' use of additional adults in the classroom, dismissing the strategy as a waste of money and poor value in terms of outcomes. What we have to say about this is that in some respects he was right. At the time there was less understanding about the role of classroom assistants and far too often they did not have a significant impact on the learning. However, what is missed far too often is the stuff that doesn't appear in a results league table: how kids feel, how well they attend, how they behave and what their aspirations are – all things on which a classroom assistant can have a major impact.

We have already alluded to the fact that we are very proud to be teachers and we readily acknowledge the role that different professionals play in schools. There are a myriad of different subtleties in the way they all interact with young people and each other. The role of the classroom assistant is like a diamond in the snow, where the light dances off different surfaces at different angles. Brilliant classroom assistants are exceptionally skilled professionals

and they deserve their place in the pantheon of adults who enrich the lives of youngsters on a daily basis.

There is no single job description that would fit the role. At primary school level, classroom assistants are often attached to a particular class and they will spend most or all of their time with that class. Alternatively, they may be appointed to support an individual student who has special educational needs. This could be a physical disability or a particular learning need, or it may be that the provision of a classroom assistant comes as a result of an education, health and care plan (EHCP). Bearing in mind what we have said about the importance of relationships, there is clearly a difference between these two functions. On the one hand we are talking about developing relationships with a whole class and the individuals in it, and on the other hand the forging of a unique relationship with one student. In the first role you will be interacting with different children throughout the day, whereas in the second you are going to be wholly focused on one child (although this does not exclude you from working with others too). In fact, classroom assistants are increasingly deployed to work with small groups of students to develop targeted skills identified by the class teacher – for example, focused literacy and numeracy, social skills work or emotional literacy.

At secondary level, the nature of the curriculum often means that the role will be different. You may be assigned to a particular subject area so that you are always on hand to support children in, say, science. Alternatively, you may be attached to a year group – so you may support kids in Year 8, travelling with them from English to maths to art. There is also, of course, provision for individual students with special educational needs and disability (SEND). It can be quite hard to establish these relationships initially because it is unusual for a classroom assistant to transfer from primary school to secondary school and 'follow' the child to a new school. This means that a student with SEND who has got used to one helper, often over a period of years, now has to adapt to a new person on arrival at senior school.

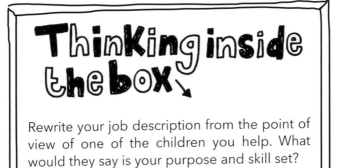

Thinking inside the box

Rewrite your job description from the point of view of one of the children you help. What would they say is your purpose and skill set?

In addition there are classroom assistants who are assigned to particular specialisms at every level. It may be that you are appointed because you speak a language other than English which is essential in a school with a large number of young people who speak that language. In special schools there are classroom assistants with a host of different skill sets, ranging from working with children with autism to attending to the physical needs of children with disabilities. There are also classroom assistants who bring expertise in individual areas of the curriculum such as modern foreign languages or PE.

So, who would want to be a classroom assistant? In the early days there was a notion, especially in primary schools, that this was a nice cosy opportunity for mums to help out in their child's school, and, of course, it was ideal for childcare because you work school hours and get the holidays. Be warned – life has moved on. The role is now altogether much more demanding and the expectations are very much higher. Being a classroom assistant is now an integral part of the learning jigsaw; it is not just a job.

Of course, it's easier to feel great if you're doing a job you love. Research suggests that whether you're engaged in your work depends on whether you view it as a job, a career or a calling. If you're doing a job, you'll feel it in the pit

of your stomach and going to work will be a chore. You're a classroom assistant because it pays the bills and you'll get that feeling of angst when the alarm goes off at stupid o'clock.

A career is a necessity but you see opportunities for success and making some sort of difference. It's up the evolutionary scale from a job and you're likely to feel you're moving in the right direction. You're invested in your work and want to do well. You might be tempted to study for a foundation degree or, as your career gathers pace, you may feel that you would like to progress further and become a higher level teaching assistant. As an HLTA, you will assume greater responsibilities, which may include working alongside the teacher to prepare units of work, and you will share greater responsibility for delivering these units to the children either in a whole class scenario or working with a small group. We have seen a number of brilliant classroom assistants relish this opportunity to develop their role further. It has given them a chance for career and personal development, and it has been of benefit to the kids as well. Plus, if you are viewing your role as a career, it may be that you are considering going the whole hog and becoming a teacher.

A calling is where the work is an end in itself. You feel fulfilled and have a sense of contribution to the greater good. Work is likely to draw

on your personal strengths and gives your life meaning and purpose. And, whisper it quietly, you'd probably do it for free.

Whether you see being a classroom assistant as a job, a career or a calling has less to do with your work than you might imagine. A calling can have just as much to do with your mindset as it does with the actual work you do. Please let us remind you of the classic story of the man who was sweeping the floor at NASA. When someone asked him what his job was, he replied, 'I'm helping put a man on the moon.'

What qualities do you need to consider when applying for a job as a classroom assistant? We believe there is one overriding requirement: you need to have a passion for working with young people, plus you need to burn with ambition to give them the very best start in life. We did once come across a classroom assistant who confessed that she didn't really like children. Forgive us, but can you spot what made us think that maybe she was in the wrong job? When we are interviewing, the one thing we look for above all else is a candidate who is child centred in their thinking and in their responses. We are looking for someone with full on commitment who will give their heart and soul to the school and the children.

Thinking inside the box

Harry Emerson Fosdick famously wrote about a summer's day during his childhood when his mother sent him out to pick a quart of raspberries. 'I dragged my feet in rebellion,' he is reported to have said, 'and the bucket was filling very slowly. Then a new idea came to me. Wouldn't it be fun to pick two quarts of raspberries and surprise her?'

So the young Harry set about his new task: 'I had such an interesting time picking those two quarts, to the utter amazement of the household, and they never forgot it. But, I have never forgotten the philosophy of it. We can change any situation by changing our attitude toward it. Nobody ever finds life worth living. One always has to make it worth living.'

Do you need any specific qualifications? The answer to this is that it may depend on the exact nature of the job description. You will certainly need to have good grades in English and maths at GCSE or equivalent. Your literacy, numeracy

and ICT skills need to be excellent because we are in the business of ensuring that children do well in those subjects that cut across all others. We compete with an incredible amount of poor language on TV and in social media, so it's important the spoken and written language of educationalists is pretty good. Some schools may require a relevant qualification in, for example, nursery work, childcare, play work or youth work. Sometimes there is no requirement for formal qualifications but the school will look for previous experience of working with young people, such as the Guides, Scouts, theatre groups or sports clubs.

A good route into becoming a classroom assistant might be to enlist as a volunteer in a school, helping out with reading or on a school trip. Schools are always keen to recruit top quality staff, but there is always a natural concern about appointing someone who is unsuitable, so the more a school knows about a candidate, the more likely they are to consider that person favourably at interview. Working as a volunteer can function as a very handy extended job interview, and we can track many outstandingly effective colleagues who have worked their way up in schools, step by step, starting with very basic volunteering roles.

So, while some relevant qualifications might get you as far as the interview room, it's your people skills that will swing it. The three things you really need to be a brilliant classroom assistant are our version of the 3 Rs: relationships, relationships and, you've guessed it, relationships. Let us assure you that not everybody is endowed with the same ability to create positive working relationships. In fact, we're beginning to think that these so-called 'soft skills' are a complete misnomer. What exactly is soft about being able to demonstrate resilience, leadership, happiness, confidence, integrity and compassion? What is soft about being able to tune into people's emotions and get on their wavelength? What is soft about being able to use these qualities to help you adapt to the constantly changing world? Soft skills? Was somebody taking the mick? These are very hard skills indeed. And you're going to need them in abundance, along with enthusiasm, passion and energy.

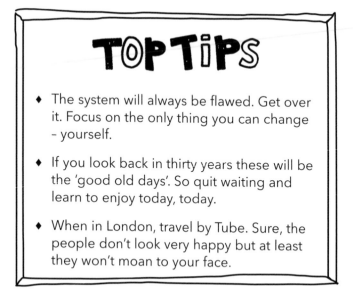

TOP TIPS

- The system will always be flawed. Get over it. Focus on the only thing you can change – yourself.

- If you look back in thirty years these will be the 'good old days'. So quit waiting and learn to enjoy today, today.

- When in London, travel by Tube. Sure, the people don't look very happy but at least they won't moan to your face.

Lesson 2

LEADING WITHOUT A TITLE

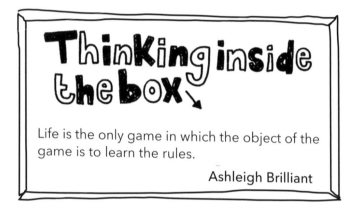

Thinking inside the box

Life is the only game in which the object of the game is to learn the rules.

Ashleigh Brilliant

When we're not teaching or playing our part in running our school, we run training courses for all of those engaged in this endlessly fascinating game of chess that is education. One of the glorious benefits of doing this is that we get to talk education with experts all the time. In case you were wondering, these 'experts' are not grey-bearded bow-tied professors who inhabit the ivory towers of academia, who know all the theories but who wouldn't know what to do on

a wet lunchtime, or if there was an outbreak of head lice, if their life depended on it. Nor are they the leaders of education who garner huge salaries for making strategic decisions but who tend to avoid walking the corridors at morning breaktime. Of course, we err on the side of cynicism here because all of these individuals play their part in the labyrinth of successful education. No, the 'experts' we refer to are those who are often the unsung heroes and heroines of schools; those who do the business in the classroom day in, day out. We have never yet come out of a training day without having learned something new ourselves.

It is deeply engrained in the mindset of everyone who works alongside children to want to improve all the time. When something hasn't gone as well as we would have wished, we all go away and instinctively think, 'How could I have done that better?' We encourage you to reflect when things have gone well too. Reflect on what you did that worked superbly and how you can tinker with it to make it even more earth shattering next time. But, in your role, it might not be that you're reflecting on a light bulb moment of learning; it could be that you've made a relationship breakthrough.

Rita Pierson suggests that children don't learn from people they don't like, so you have to get the children on your side first. Think 'hearts' and 'minds' in that order.[1]

So, the big questions are, 'What works?' and 'How can we play a significant role in improving outcomes for children?' We know that politicians often reach for the lever which says 'school structures', 'new buildings', 'a reformed national curriculum' or 'harder exams', but for us it is back to basics. What *really* makes a difference? At the very hub of it all it is the quality of the relationships between those who lead the learning and the kids which allows great learning to take place. And that means both the teacher and the classroom assistant.

---

1 Rita Pierson, Every Kid Needs a Champion, *TED.com* (May 2013). Available at: https://www.ted.com/talks/rita_pierson_every_kid_needs_a_champion?language=en.

Some years ago we were conducting some research into really inspirational educators when we came across this famous quote by Haim Ginott:

I've come to the frightening conclusion that I am the decisive element in the classroom. It's my personal approach that creates the climate. It's my daily mood that makes the weather. As a teacher I possess a tremendous power to make a child's life miserable or joyous. I can be a tool of torture or an instrument of inspiration. I can humiliate or humor, hurt or heal. In all situations, it is my response that decides whether a crisis will be escalated or de-escalated, and a child humanized or de-humanized.[2]

We think that this is so fundamental to everything we do as educators that it should be on the back of every staff toilet door in every school, so that even in those most private of moments (which are extremely rare on a school day) the very essence of what we are about is encapsulated. We need to forgive Ginott for only making mention of the teacher. He left us for the great staffroom in the sky in 1973 when classroom assistants were still unknown, but as he looks

---

2 Haim Ginott, *Teacher and Child: A Book for Parents and Teachers* (New York: Macmillan, 1971).

I've come to the frightening conclusion that I am the decisive element in the classroom. It's my personal approach that creates the climate. It's my daily mood that makes the weather. As a teacher I possess a tremendous power to make a child's life miserable or joyous. I can be a tool of torture or an instrument of inspiration. I can humiliate or humor, hurt or heal. In all situations, it is my response that decides whether a crisis will be escalated or de-escalated, and a child humanized or de-humanized.

This should be on the back of every staff toilet door!

down on us from his celestial staffroom, he will nod in approval at the addition of a whole new layer of experts to help children learn.

It is easy to argue that the classroom assistant is even more of a 'decisive element' than the teacher. You might be focused on one or two children and, let's not beat about the bush, you are having a profound impact on their learning and their lives. You really can't get more decisive than that.

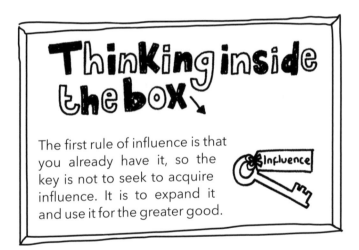

Thinking inside the box

The first rule of influence is that you already have it, so the key is not to seek to acquire influence. It is to expand it and use it for the greater good.

We've found that it depends on what type of day you're having as to which part of Ginott's quote speaks to you at any one point in time. We recently watched an outstandingly

dedicated classroom assistant work with a child called Aiden. He already carries the label of 'challenging' – Aiden loathes maths, he hates school and he doesn't like teachers, any of them. Aiden is the latest in a long line of older brothers and sisters who all fitted the same mould. It is not looking good, especially when Aiden is told that the lesson is about calculating area. This is only one of the topics that Aiden will encounter during the day which he will take a nanosecond to dismiss as 'boring'. The next step is, usually, that Aiden will be disruptive, which in turn means he will be reprimanded, which in turn means he gets angry. You can see where this is heading: Aiden is about to disrupt the entire class and let his loathing of maths rob twenty-nine other children of the opportunity to develop a love of maths.

Switch off your automatic judge-ometer. You know the one – the inner voice that makes assumptions about everyone and everything. The likelihood is that your judge-ometer is set to 'snap judgement mode'. As Ellen Langer

says, 'we are frequently in error but rarely in doubt'.[3] Before you engage with anyone, take four seconds, in your head, to send warmth and love to that person.

Switch off your automatic Judge-ometer!

But here's the magical bit. The classroom assistant who works with Aiden knows all the indicators and she immediately side-tracked him into a discussion about a new carpet in her lounge. She began by laughing because they couldn't get the long roll of carpet around the corner of her hall easily and had, in the process, knocked off the main carpet fitter's glasses. She made it sound like a slapstick sketch. Once engaged in considering the problems the fitters had in cutting out a piece of carpet of the appropriate size to fit around the fireplace, Aiden is now being coaxed into thinking about how to calculate the area involved. Aiden was on the cusp of being awkward, rebellious and truculent – and, of course, learning nothing. The

3   Ellen J. Langer, *On Becoming An Artist: Reinventing Yourself Through Mindful Creativity* (New York: Random House, 2005), p. 11.

teacher has at least six children in the class who could reasonably pass as doppelgängers for Aiden, certainly in terms of their attitude to learning. Her hands were already full.

The classroom assistant could have taken a negative, critical or 'telling off' approach. This would have resulted in a spiral of negativity which would have represented torture for Aiden, rendering him even more miserable. Instead, she used her power to engage and inspire him. Okay, we might stop just short of saying he was 'joyous', but he was on board, he was learning in a context which he could identify with, see the point of and, thus, he was no bother to anyone else. Pure gold from that classroom assistant – brilliant. She was the decisive element.

Classroom assistants, like teachers, perform daily miracles. What was it that humanised Aiden? The fact that he attends an academy? The fact that his school had recently had a £1.3 million refit? His shiny new electronic registration system? No, just total brilliance from his classroom assistant. The teacher on her own could not have achieved the same effect.

This is such a powerful moment, so let's just hammer home the full impact of it. Aiden is engaged and does some learning about a subject he thinks he hates, so he's a winner. The other twenty-nine children get to knuckle down and learn about maths, so they're winners. The

teacher has a relieved smile on her face – her lesson's gone according to plan (*woo-hoo*) – so she's a winner. That smile continues when she walks through her front door, so her family are winners (stop us when you're getting bored). Aiden has had a decent day at school, so when he gets home his mum's a winner. The head teacher hasn't had to call Aiden into her office today, so she's mightily relieved and has managed to clear some emails. She fist-pumps her way across the car park at 6 p.m. – *early finish* – another winner. And all of this can be traced back to a piece of magic by the classroom assistant. This moment created a ripple effect that goes far beyond the classroom. How powerful is that? Truly amazing classroom assistants do this day in, day out.

Let's share another example. We were with Iona recently. Iona attends a special school and has multiple challenges, most notably difficulties with people she doesn't know. On the day we spent with her, not only were we present but there was also another boy, Jack, who was new to the class. Iona seemed particularly unsettled at one stage during the morning and was becoming more and more agitated by the presence of Jack.

The teacher was preoccupied with two other students, so it was the classroom assistant who took charge. Knowing that Iona was always

interested in a specially made board into which different materials had been inlaid, all of which provided different sensory experiences, the classroom assistant took both Iona and Jack over to the board and encouraged Iona to feel the roughness of the lumps of stone, then the smoothness of the marble followed by the warmth of the polished wood. Iona was soon absorbed by this because it is one of her favourite parts of the classroom. The crisis had been de-escalated. Iona was calm and reassured and was soon smiling at Jack who was also invited to experience the different textures. By the end of the day the two were working jointly on a textile project and were laughing together. That wonderfully skilled and committed classroom assistant had not only de-escalated the potential crisis but had played a huge role in humanising those young people. It was the start of yet another ripple.

Here are a few more illustrations, just so the penny drops. In a primary school numeracy lesson, Cayden was struggling with simple subtraction using single digit numbers. His classroom assistant helped him to make substantial strides forward by using Polo mints, coins and ping-pong balls, which was particularly inspired because Cayden made a beeline for the ping-pong table in the playground as soon as the first ding-dong of the bell announcing morning breaktime was heard.

Still with numeracy, Owen suddenly made a giant leap in his learning when his classroom assistant helped him to learn his four times table. He knew Owen was into cricket and asked him to calculate the score of his favourite Test match batsman if he hit the first three balls of the match for a boundary, then the first four balls and so on. In both cases, the classroom assistant used what the child was interested in to advance the learning.

In her special school, Mollie was learning about colours. She was a very tactile, kinaesthetic learner so her classroom assistant brought in balloons of all the different colours. Together they used a marker pen to write the colours on each balloon which helped Mollie to remember the spellings as well as the colours.

Lianne had never been able to catch a ball in PE but her classroom assistant worked with her using different sized balls, starting with a huge beach ball, and created a game with a scoring system akin to one Lianne knew from a popular television game show. She loved it and was so keen on beating her own record that her competence and confidence grew progressively throughout the lesson.

All of these brilliant classroom assistants came up with ideas which were a little bit quirky and different to help these kids learn. In some cases they had come up with their own resources.

They discussed them with the teachers they worked with and then embedded them into the learning. Some even went beyond that and gave up extra time after school and at lunchtime for these young people. The impact of their input was immediately measurable. It was also noticeable that they had all clearly planned in advance how they were going to approach the lesson, having previously consulted with the teacher on the learning objectives. Cleverly, they enabled the children to discover the learning for themselves.

Thinking inside the box

If a child is struggling to come up with an answer try asking, 'If you did know the answer, what would it be?' This accesses their subconscious mind. The chances are that it's hidden in there somewhere and this question will bring it to the surface.

If you add these examples together, you'll find that the collective brilliance of classroom assistants creates not just a ripple but a tsunami of a difference. Robin Sharma talks about 'leading without a title', or LWT, by which he means that it's not just leaders who lead.[4] Your job title is therefore misleading. To us, a brilliant classroom assistant is a leader of learning and a role model of positivity. You might not have 'leader' in your job title, but all the previous examples prove that is exactly what you are.

In Ginott's quote, it is teachers who 'make the weather'. Bringing it up to date, Carol Dweck's research into fixed and growth mindsets is very in vogue. She talks of 'dandelion' and 'orchid' children.[5] If you are even remotely green-fingered, you'll be aware that dandelions flourish anywhere and everywhere. They're hardy and take very little nurturing. A bit of sunshine and, boom, they're out. Analogising to children, dandelions will take very little looking after and will flourish in almost all conditions.

The chances are, as a classroom assistant, you will be in charge of the opposite – the orchid children. We have an orchid in a pot on our windowsill. It requires special orchid food and,

---

4 Robin Sharma, Powerful Tactics to Lead Without a Title (30 August 2011). Available at: http://www.robinsharma.com/blog/tag/lead-without-a-title/.

5 Carol S. Dweck, *Mindset: The New Psychology of Success* (New York: Random House, 2006).

even then, a slight over- or under-watering will result in it looking very sad indeed. But if we get the care package right the orchid will, once in a blue moon, produce the most amazing flowers. The point being that orchid children require special care and attention and will only ever flourish if the climate and conditions are spot on. This can be a very difficult environment to create and a lot of over- or under-attention will make them very sad too. But, hey, if you get it right, you will be rewarded with the most spec-tacular bloom ever. But, like the orchid on our windowsill, if we stop and gloat about our great gardening skills, the damn thing wilts the very next day.

In essence, then, teachers are supposed to teach and that means classroom assistants … assist. Brilliant classroom assistants enable teachers to concentrate on teaching by helping with the classroom climate. They are the super-heroes of the educational world.[6] They meet

6 Pants on the outside are optional.

and greet the children at the beginning of the session. They help to make sure the resources are ready, the books are given out and that supplementary equipment is at hand. They know exactly where to find spare rulers and pens, and they are adept not only at handing them out but also collecting them back in again.

Brilliant classroom assistants always know instinctively when to distribute books, worksheets or equipment. There is a skill to this. Hand them out too early and the children fiddle with them and don't listen. Hand them out too late and there is a hiatus which allows the distracted to become even more distracted. They have an immediate feel for all the requirements of effective and efficient classroom management, and they act on their own initiative. They do not wait to be asked – they sense what needs to be done and they do it. It's an interesting point to note that not only will these small acts of going the extra mile make your own day brighter but they will be noticed by the children themselves. Just as children can reel off the names of good and bad teachers, so too with classroom assistants.

Brilliant classroom assistants have antennae which enable them to intervene and offer support promptly. They often pick up on the child who is unwell or who genuinely needs the toilet

and will deal with it. They can sense when a child is getting fidgety or is annoying another individual. They see when frustration has set in and a child is about to give up. However, they not only have a shrewd anticipation of when to intervene but they also know when a learner needs some space. This is especially noticeable with teenage boys. Males are delicate creatures and their pride is important to them. (We know – we are those delicate creatures!) It doesn't do their street cred a lot of good to be always under the wing of a 'mother hen', so skilled classroom assistants know when to leave well alone, as well as when to go to the rescue.

Chris and Gary flew back from a recent jaunt overseas (how stimulating it is to be able to exchange thoughts and ideas on education with other experts who work in an entirely different context) and neither of us is that enamoured about flying. As we boarded our plane, we were both bowled over by the welcome. Smiling staff greeted us as we embarked. Once we were seated, cabin staff passed among us dispensing good cheer, making two ordinary school teachers from Leicester feel as though they were the most important people on the plane. Once we were safely airborne, refreshments were dispensed from the trolley and nothing seemed too much trouble (the double gin and tonic helped, of course!). The cabin crew had managed to create a climate on board that

aircraft which was positive, reassuring and a pleasure to be a part of. They did indeed 'make the weather'.

How does that experience accord with the world of education? What part do classroom assistants play in all of this? Alongside the teacher they have a vital role to play in making young people feel appreciated, respected and valued. From the moment the children step into the learning area, whether it is the PE changing room, the drama studio or the science lab, classroom assistants are pivotal in sending out positive messages to them. Tell the children it is great to see them. Tell them they've got some really great learning activities lined up. Tell them they're going to be successful. Remind them of something they succeeded at in their last lesson. Focus on being positive no matter what. Behave as you would like them to behave.

And remember, you are the 'decisive element'.

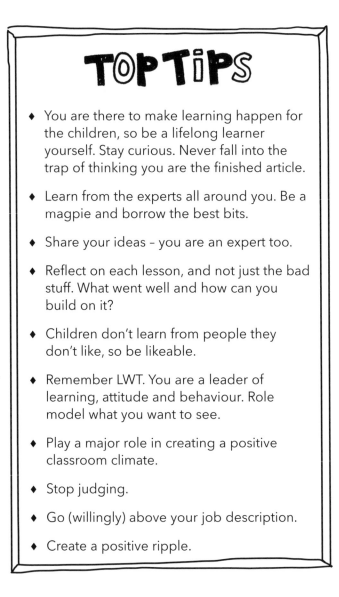

TOP TIPS

- ◆ You are there to make learning happen for the children, so be a lifelong learner yourself. Stay curious. Never fall into the trap of thinking you are the finished article.

- ◆ Learn from the experts all around you. Be a magpie and borrow the best bits.

- ◆ Share your ideas – you are an expert too.

- ◆ Reflect on each lesson, and not just the bad stuff. What went well and how can you build on it?

- ◆ Children don't learn from people they don't like, so be likeable.

- ◆ Remember LWT. You are a leader of learning, attitude and behaviour. Role model what you want to see.

- ◆ Play a major role in creating a positive classroom climate.

- ◆ Stop judging.

- ◆ Go (willingly) above your job description.

- ◆ Create a positive ripple.

Lesson 3

THE 3 Rs

Thinking inside the box ↘

Name the five wealthiest people in the world. Name the last five FA Cup winners. Name the last five winners of *The X Factor*. Name ten people who have won the Nobel Prize. Can you recall the last half dozen Academy Award winners for best actor and actress?

The point is, none of us remember the head-liners of yesterday even though they are the best in their fields. So let's try a different quiz.

List a few teachers who aided your journey through school. Name three friends who have helped you through a difficult time and five people who have taught you something worth-while. Think of a few people who have made you feel appreciated and special and five people you enjoy spending time with.

> Easier? The lesson is that the people who make the most difference in your life are not the ones with the most credentials, the most money or the most awards. They simply are the ones who care the most.

We all have certain facts which have been imprinted in our memories through repetition. Andy automatically knows what 6 x 6 is. Chris knows the capital of Spain and the year of the Battle of Hastings. Gary knows that YUP 828L was the registration plate of his dad's Vauxhall Viva in 1972. We all have similar collections. They're all etched in our minds.

Ideas and beliefs are the same. They're just things you've been told over and over again until they've become embedded. Now, don't think Chris is ever going to dislodge Barcelona or 1066 from his head. Once things are in there it's very difficult to get them out again. The upgraded version of you has to be open to new ideas and new ways of thinking. The new version of you is a green shoot and needs nurturing to the point where you can drown out the old weeds.

And this is where things get interesting – your self-image is a belief. Oh my gosh, it's not real? You are real enough but the *idea* of who you are

has been formed over your lifetime. The image you have of you has become imprinted on your subconscious and it's taken on a life of its own. In essence, you have become your own self-image. That's why confident people act confidently. That's why when Andy was told he was rubbish at maths at age 10, he still thinks he is rubbish at maths at age 48.

The previous couple of paragraphs are short on words but huge in importance. Without blinding you with the reasoning behind them, trust us when we say that they are the cornerstone of this chapter which is, in turn, the cornerstone of this book.

You've already cottoned on, haven't you? *Relationships* form the backbone of this book. They're so crucial that we've devoted a whole chapter to them but before we go there, let's visit those 'good old days' once more.

Back in the day, when Gary had his first car, he could open the bonnet and have a good look around at the various bits and bobs. He's not much of a grease monkey but he knew how to check his spark plugs and clean his tappets. Now when you pop the hood of a modern car it's a gleaming silver thing. Has it got spark plugs? We wonder if the garage even knows because when our cars go in for a service they simply plug them into a laptop and download a whole load of data (we think). The old style

mechanic had blue overalls, battered knuckles and was covered in oil, whereas the newfangled breed are disturbingly pristine.

The point is that in the olden days we would tinker under the bonnet and be able to fix things. The thinking was that if we knew how to repair things it would save calling in an expert. So think of this chapter as tinkering under the hood of the human being. We're going to have a go at lifting the lid on some of the workings of the mind that knock us off our feel-good pedestal. Fear not, it's not an in depth look at neurology. We will avoid mentioning your corpus callosum or basal ganglia. But let's have a good look around and see if we can tidy things up a bit so you can function much better. If you learn how your own relationship engine works, it might help to prevent you having a breakdown and getting stuck on the hard shoulder of life.

We had an interesting experience recently during a school trip in which we asked a series of questions presented in a format which was

readily identifiable to the kids from a well-known television show. One of the questions invited them to think of teachers who had long hair. It was a good wheeze which entertained us hugely because they thought almost exclusively of female teachers, and when we revealed some of the correct answers, as chosen in our survey, there was a look of wonderment when we mentioned two male teachers with long hair. However, what was even more interesting was that the two names who got a lot of airplay were, in fact, classroom assistants.

What does this tell us? In the eyes of children, there is no discernible difference between teachers and classroom assistants. Both are regarded as being of equal status. Our business is helping people to be brilliant, to be the best version of themselves that they can possibly be, and the first thing to keep in mind is that the revolution has to start with ourselves.

So how do we define 'brilliant'? Well, we could waffle on using the terminology which frequents performance management reviews or turn to the pages of the most recent Ofsted guidance, but as you have hopefully gathered by now, that is not our style. It is easier than that: ask the kids. And, if you do, this is what they will say, as reported by Steve Munby, chief

executive of CfBT Education Trust (now Education Development Trust). This, according to your 'customers', is what makes great learning:

My teacher believes that all students can do well.

My teacher believes that learning is important.

My teacher seems to like teaching.

My teacher expects me to do well.

My teacher is interested in what the students think.[1]

We're on very safe territory if we substitute 'teacher' with 'classroom assistant'. Now look here, folks, it's not our fault that our customers have stated the bleedin' obvious. We're suspecting you already knew the points above. But how many can you hand-on-heartedly tick?

And herein lies the conundrum of being a world class classroom assistant. The solutions are simple. There are no ifs and buts about those five points above, but 'simple' doesn't mean 'easy'. The chances are you have been handed the

1   Steve Munby, Learning Centred Leadership, keynote speech delivered at the Inspiring Leadership Conference, June 2014. Available at: http://cdn.cfbt.com/~/media/CfBTCorporate/Files/Resources/inspiring-leadership-2014/keynote-Steve-Munby-Inspiring-Leadership-Speech.pdf.

challenge of bringing out the best in some of the most difficult to engage children, with whom even the Dalai Lama would struggle to remain positive. But we're back to good and bad exhaustion. You're pretty much guaranteed to be spent at the end of each day – all that emotional giving can deplete you. If you've been on autopilot, going through the motions and not really caring about the children or their learning, you will be exhausted for all the wrong reasons. But if you truly go for it, and along with those five points above, you operate the 'Pygmalion effect', you will get home knackered but fulfilled. You have given your all for a good cause.

←The Pygmalion effect?

But what was that we said in the previous sentence – something about pigs? The Pygmalion effect is a subconscious phenomenon whereby people live up or down to the expectations we have of them. It all happens below the radar, so to speak. So, you might not be consciously aware of it but if, for example, a child arrives in your class and his older sister or brother had given the school a hard time, it's incredibly

difficult to give that child a clean slate. You will have emotional baggage, and the Pygmalion effect means that the child will live down to your low expectations.

Let's give you an example. Andy is currently working on a project aimed at staff in children's homes. While 38% of Year 13s nationally go on to higher education, just 6% of teenagers from children's homes go to university,[2] and the thinking is that it is largely due to the subconscious messages they receive. Although those who work with the children genuinely care for them and want them to do well, the subliminal message that the young people are hearing is, 'Poor kids from broken homes and terrible backgrounds. You don't stand a chance.' We hope to God nobody is actually saying those words but, nevertheless, that is the overriding message they're picking up.

So press the reset button on your expectations. Raise them. Andy has a phrase that he uses on INSET days – 'everything speaks' – and by that he means that it's not just what you say that the children are

---

2 See http://www.thewhocarestrust.org.uk/pages/the-statistics.html.

listening to, it's the way you say it. Your body language is screaming a message. Your face. Your clothes too. The classroom is also 'speaking' to the children and telling them what to expect. In short, everything about you and your classroom is giving a message. So please, for the sake of the children, let the message be 'high expectations'.

Chris and Gary are sufficiently experienced (i.e. old codgers) to be able to apply the thirty year test. Thirty years on you are highly likely to meet people who once upon a time you helped with their learning. This will be challenging for you. You look exactly the same, naturally. Well, of course you do – you haven't got a grey hair on your head, you've still got hair and you haven't put on weight. You are, in your mind at least, the eternal Peter Pan. They, on the other hand, look entirely different. They are adults for a start and may have accompanying partners or children with them. Much as they peer at you and say invitingly, 'Hello, Miss. Do you remember me?' you probably haven't got a clue who they are. We have decided that it's better to admit defeat on this one. Rather than clutching at straws, and finding out they are the wrong straws in attempting to identify your mystery assailant in the local supermarket, we have found that they are usually very understanding if you ply the line of, 'I

do recognise your face but, forgive me, with several thousand to choose from, I'm struggling to put a name to the face.'

Once the opening formalities are completed, you then enter the zone of reminiscences, and this is where the brilliant classroom assistants stand apart from the ordinary. If they have fond memories of you, the stories will come tumbling out. To some degree they will remember the things you did or said, but what will underpin all of this is how you made them feel. Go back to the 'decisive element' quote. Did you humour or heal? Did you inspire or make their life joyous? Were you the person who made them believe they could enjoy success? Were you the one who made them feel special? Were you the one who encouraged them? Were you the one who made them feel valued and respected? Were you the one who made them understand that coming to school was a good thing?

We met Georgina recently who was serving in a restaurant where we were having a meal with six other members of staff. She was startled when Chris said, 'Hello Georgina', and clearly impressed that he'd remembered her name (he hadn't, it was on her badge). We were not absolutely convinced that she wholly enjoyed seeing a whole phalanx of her former teachers during her shift. She recognised one of us and greeted us with formal politeness before realising that

there were seven others in tow. However, conversation ensued and we asked if she had any happy memories from school. She pondered for a moment before saying to one of the classroom assistants present, 'I used to like it when you came into our lessons to help me. You were the only person who was nice to me.' She had forgotten what this colleague had done, she had forgotten what she had said, but she hadn't forgotten how she had been made to feel. The sign of a brilliant classroom assistant. If they remember you like this in thirty years' time, you have passed the test.

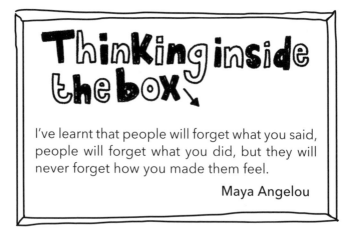

I've learnt that people will forget what you said, people will forget what you did, but they will never forget how you made them feel.

Maya Angelou

So what are the magic ingredients? Over the years we have worked with classroom assistants who get the children eating out of their hands and we have seen others who struggle to get learners on board. What is the difference, the magic elixir? We put it to you that the difference lies in the relationship between the classroom assistant and the kids.

Let's start with some general stuff before homing in on how it applies in the classroom. First up, what is your default setting: setting 1, 'passive bystander' or setting 2, 'active and engaged'?

You might think that we're born with the factory default of setting 2. We don't know any children who sit passively on their first birthday, surrounded by crinkly wrapping paper, looking bored. They toss the toys aside and get stuck into crinkling, tearing and eating the stuff. And the boxes that the toys came in? Well, they're now a rocket or a pirate ship ('Hoist the mainsail, Jim lad!') If Andy goes to the park with his 2-year-old niece, it's a massive adventure and she insists on jumping in every puddle and chasing every duck. She has rosy cheeks, sparkly eyes, infinite curiosity and oodles of glee. Sure, it might be partly fuelled by her chocolatey breakfast cereal, but what if it's a bit deeper than that? What if we all have access to that inner source of inspiration and energy? To mix

our breakfast cereal metaphors, your internal snap, crackle and pop shows on the outside in the fabled Ready Brek glow.

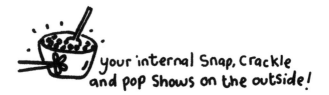

your internal Snap, Crackle and pop Shows on the outside!

And then, somewhere along the line, we become inert and uninterested. Flat. Maybe even a little lost. Life somehow loses its lustre. We end up feeling like cereal that's had the milk poured on ages ago and our snap, crackle and pop has become a soggy mush. The spring in your step is a slouch. The twinkle in your eye is a sty. We get eroded. Scientists call it 'habituation' and it's so gradual that you often don't notice. Your work isn't quite as exciting, your partner isn't quite as attractive and you have become a bit stale with the children.

But hang on, if we were born 'active and engaged', then surely that's our default position? So, when did jumping into a cardboard box with a swashbuckling cry of 'Ahoy there me hearties!' become inappropriate? Can you remember the exact time when jumping in puddles became a bad idea? When did you last go

to the park and chase the ducks, squealing with glee? And when did working with kids become a chore?

We appreciate that human beings are incredibly complex animals, but have you noticed that when a complicated piece of technology goes wrong it always has a button that sets it back to its default factory setting? What if we could do the same? Thinking aloud, maybe fun, giggly, playful and 'Walk the plank yer rotten scoundrel' is our factory setting, but somehow we forgot along the way? Surely, that would mean personal development is dead in the water and all you need is a huge spoonful of 'personal remembering'.

In order for people to buy into you, you need to come alive. This is a bigger deal than you might imagine because, look around you, what do you see? A lot of worn-out staff counting down to the weekend, half-term or retirement. So, imagine you had a thermostat in the middle of your chest and you can choose a setting of 'Can't be arsed' at one end and 'Ahoy there me hearties' at the other. Turn the dial. Not so that you scare the living day-lights out of people, but dare to turn it so that you are a joy and pleasure to be

'Ahoy there me hearties'

Turn the dial

'Can't be arsed'

with. There should always be a smile, energy and genuine interest in the child you are supporting.

It can be quite a brave position to take because you will stand out a mile.

This week on Monday and Tuesday, really go for it. Be your true self and unleash your true and total personality on the world. Take action, enjoy life to the full, see the very best in everything and everybody, and help others to do the same. Surround yourself with positive people (this will happen automatically, because when other people can do something them- selves, or believe they can, they want to tell you that you can too), smile when you see the sun, laugh when you feel happy, bubble with love, energy and the thrill of being alive.

On the Wednesday and Thursday, go for noth- ing. Be that impostor who inhabits your thoughts and body, do nothing, complain a lot and say that life has got it in for you, bring oth- ers down by telling them how you feel.

Surround yourself with negative people (this will happen automatically, because when other people can't do something themselves, or believe they can't, they want to tell you that you can't either). Frown when you see the sun, cry when you feel sad, freeze with fear and the nightmare of existence.

And on the Friday ask yourself this single question - which of these two days did I enjoy more?

If it was the Monday and Tuesday - live like that every day.

If it was the Wednesday and Thursday - live like that every day.

David Taylor[3]

Of course, this is general advice rather than classroom specific. Trying to live life to the fullest, rather than just getting by, means you will shift to what Andy calls 'healthy functioning' - and it's contagious. It attracts and engages others. Some people are naturals in their positive outlook, others might require a bit of extra help, but we're all capable of it.

3 David Taylor, *The Naked Coach: Business Coaching Made Simple* (Chichester: Capstone, 2007), pp. 72-73.

However, the more we learn, the less inclined we are to suggest that we need to take responsibility for other people's happiness. It's quite empowering to realise that we don't have to carry that burden. At first blush this next sentence sounds controversial: we can't 'fix' anyone. All we can do is take charge of our own thoughts and let our best self shine. That way, you stand a chance of lighting up a few others.

"I changed my thoughts and started to SHINE."

Your job is not to inspire anyone else, it's to be inspired.

Let's delve a bit deeper into the murky world of emotions. Emotions are feelings and they're right here, slap bang in the middle of your awareness. They are extremely variable and, in theory at least, controllable. That's because emotions aren't 'real'. By that, we mean emotions don't have a form or a shape. You can't put your emotions in a wheelbarrow and cart them around. They're a mental construct in your head. *You* created them.

We have four hard-wired emotional programmes that Steven Pinker calls the 4 Fs: feeding, fighting, fleeing and, ahem, sexual behaviour.[4] All of which are primitive impulses that come from the depths of our evolution – reptilian thinking, if you like. These programmes are basically about the survival of the species,

---

4   Steven Pinker, *How the Mind Works* (New York: W.W. Norton, 1997).

and as the human mammal evolved they stuck around and have been bequeathed to us as part of the Neolithic brain package. Although we've learned to control them, they go some of the way to explaining why plenty of folks still lean towards leopard print knickers.

(My Faves! #Kinky

Then a new layer of brain was bolted on, right at the front. The neocortex serves two useful purposes. First, it allows you to keep your hat on and, second, it provides some regulation of the 4 Fs. So, a few hundred thousand years ago the human brain was upgraded with extra capacity, a bit like a new operating system. And it's this bit that raises us above, say, squirrels. In the autumn, the squirrel population doesn't all of a sudden think, 'Mmmm, those snowy days will soon be here so I'd better bury a few nuts to ward off the winter hunger.' The squirrel doesn't rationalise as humans do. Its brain notices the days are getting shorter and our furry chum simply responds to its primitive nut-burying instinct. It doesn't really know why.

Our superior brains give us massive processing power but they are also constructed to facilitate the transfer of emotions. Social intelligence means that emotions are viral. Your emotional system is open – rather like a Wi-Fi signal that is out there for others to log on to. And this is where it gets messy because there is no password protection, so we're all logging on to each other. That's why, in a class of thirty children, it can become very emotionally draining because you're logging on to all those neural Wi-Fi networks.

Daniel Goleman calls it an 'emotional tango' – a show of emotion that works best when it's co-ordinated with those around you.[5] If we drop the Wi-Fi analogy, the science is actually straightforward. We have a set of neural mirrors which means we copy others' emotions and behaviours. These 'mirror neurons' allow contagion, letting the feelings we witness flow through us, thus helping us to get in synch with the person feeling the emotion. This ability to 'feel' with and for them is the basis of empathy. It also gives us a set of social skills that enables us to make appropriate and timely emotional responses. Empathy is used in three distinct senses: knowing another person's feelings, feeling what that person feels and responding appropriately to their feelings.

---

5   Daniel Goleman, *Social Intelligence: The New Science of Human Relationships* (London: Arrow, 2007), p. 5.

Mirror neurons are also essential in helping children to learn. They watch and copy. Mum smiles and the baby smiles back. Similarly, an enthusiastic classroom assistant creates enthusiasm in their learners. To understand someone else, mirror neurons allow us to experience their love, hatred, joy, anger, dismay, hilarity, whatever. If you think about it, it's a rather sophisticated form of subconscious communication. Daniel Stern nails it, suggesting that our nervous systems are 'constructed to be captured by the nervous systems of others, so we can experience others as if from within their skin'.[6] So, at an unconscious level we are in constant dialogue with everyone with whom we interact.

Now, here's where it gets especially pertinent. Mirror neurons have a special feature: a power dynamic is in play so that emotions flow with special strength from the more socially dominant person to the less. So, in plain simple English, if you can remain upbeat and positive, even in the face of provocation, your emotional dominance will triumph. That means it's worth putting a modicum of effort into maintaining your positivity and enthusiasm. Yes, we

---

6 Daniel N. Stern, *The Present Moment in Psychotherapy and Everyday Life* (New York: W.W. Norton, 2004), p. 76, cited in Goleman, *Social Intelligence*, p. 43.

appreciate that it can be very difficult to maintain your brilliance if the children have lost theirs, but we never said this was easy. Simple, yes. Easy, no.

But here's the clincher - remember leading without a title. Goleman also suggests that a leader's emotions have a dominant effect. So yourself and the teacher, as leaders of the classroom, have a disproportionate effect on the mood of the children. This is the last time we will mention the 'decisive element' but, we promise you, this really is it. Your emotions are truly creating the emotional climate.

Two huge points leap out of this. First, if you (the leader) are downbeat and pessimistic, thirty children will log on and catch that signal. Ditto positive and enthusiastic. Your choice. Second, and a teensie bit controversially, one of the most important roles you can play is helping to maintain the teacher's positivity and confidence. It's all well and good doing a superb job with the children, but a world class assistant will also go out of their way to catch the teacher doing things well and have a positive debrief at the end of the lesson. Or simply a nice comment on the way out the door - 'Awesome lesson, beautifully planned and delivered.' In a bizarre,

open-access Wi-Fi kind of way, an upbeat and confident teacher will inspire the children, which will in turn make your job a whole lot easier.

Thinking inside the box

In a University of Cardiff study, women who received Botox injections were unable to frown and ended up feeling happier.[7] (Please note, this is not a top tip, merely an observation about how your body language affects your emotions.)

The hallmark of a really effective classroom assistant is their ability to engage with kids who are hard to engage. It is an unwritten law of working in education that when you first arrive in post, young people will want to test you out. They will want to push at the frontiers to see what you are made of. Some will give you a

---

7 See Cosmetic Injections Depression Link, *BBC News* (11 April 2013). Available at: http://www.bbc.co.uk/news/health-22106569.

fairly easy ride and will be quick to see what you have to offer and will want to engage with you. Others will not.

It might be worth considering for a moment why they are reluctant to engage. Guess what, in the same way that we say they are hard going, it is highly likely that they will say they find us hard going as well. There could be multiple reasons for this:

♦ We are adults with a very different experience of the world to them.

♦ They have negative adult role models at home.

♦ Their role models are not interested in school and readily express their views on it.

♦ We represent just another raft of adults in an area where they are not interested and not successful.

♦ This kind of adult is associated with telling them off and punishing them.

♦ This kind of adult does not listen.

♦ They do not feel valued or respected by this kind of adult.

♦ They don't get the point of school (e.g. 'There aren't any jobs anyway').

In some senses the newly arrived classroom assistant is guilty by association, so first base is to debunk this sort of mythology. You have to get them in your pocket. But how? Once you start to make them feel good about their learning and their progress, you will have got off on the right foot. So how can you develop these relationships further? Make sure you have at the forefront of your mind in every interaction the outcome you want. Next time, are they more likely to want to do what you want them to do?

Think back to page 47 and that question we asked you about your own teachers. We're sure you will have had a favourite. Was it the Year 5 teacher who realised you are awesome at art? Was it the science teacher who understood why you were struggling to get that experiment to work? Was it the history teacher who inspired you by doing a Winston Churchill voice when you were learning about the Second World War? Was it the art teacher who showed you how to draw a cartoon successfully? Once you start to dig a little deeper into why you worshipped the ground of that particular teacher, you will probably find ingredients like he or she was 'funny' or 'made me feel I could do it'.

Humour is a key ingredient in building relationships. A young naval officer we knew[8] was given his first command of a group of thirty

8 It was actually Chris's dad.

hard-bitten, battle-hardened stokers (the men who live in the bottom of the ship and, in the days of steam, fuelled the engine with coal) with these instructions: 'You've got six weeks to get to know every one of them, what makes them tick and, most importantly of all, how to make them laugh.' The same maxim applies to teachers and classroom assistants.

Get to know your kids, each and every one of the ones you work with. What makes them tick? Can you make them laugh? The silver lining of working with children who may be hard going is that once you forge that relationship, they will give you the most extraordinary loyalty. This will be worth gold dust to you on the day of the Ofsted inspection or when you are under the weather with the flu.

We have spent a lot of time musing on the difference between the way boys and girls learn. It is the stuff of stand-up comedians to muse on the apparently unbridgeable chasm which exists between the genders. Aside from the conventional wisdom that men cannot multi-task, one of our favourites is that 'men will never be able to compete with chocolate'. The bearded and bow-tied educationalists have delved into the different approaches to learning for boys and girls, but something we have observed repeatedly is that boys need to 'get' the teacher or the classroom assistant before

they will allow that person to work with them. This is vital because boys are overrepresented among those who classroom assistants work with.

Recalling the advice given to that young naval officer ('Get to know every one of them, what makes them tick …') is where mini-conversations come in. Effective classroom assistants *really* know their kids. They take care to do their background research, talking to the class teacher or the form tutor to find out as much as they can about the students. They know if one of the children they work with has got a new baby in the family, is into Formula 1, which football team they support, whether they follow certain programmes on TV, if they have a new bike, whether they got their new piece of IT kit for Christmas – in fact, they find out everything they can about each student.

This acts as a way into a mini-conversation in which you touch base with the child you work with, either in the classroom or out and about. It need not be a prolonged exchange and it should be entirely on your terms. But it is incredibly powerful to say to a child in the dining hall, 'Great race on Sunday – I didn't think he would overtake on that last bend', and then move on. It is equally effective to say to a child as they arrive for a lesson, 'Your new bike looks like a mean machine' and, yes, follow it up with

a high five if you want. As you both get your books out, it's good to be able to have a quick exchange on the weekend's football results before moving on. This is not an in depth discussion; it is a quick acknowledgement of their world before settling down to work. It doesn't even require a response from them.

The purpose is to send a subconscious signal to them that they matter, that what they are into is important and valued. It leaves them with the subliminal message that says, 'This person is interested in me.' The outcome? Hopefully, over time, this will help you to form the kind of relationship with them that makes them want to do what you want them to do. For the boys, in particular, this is a vital part of whether they 'get' you or not.

In Andy's research he came across a Gallup survey that, despite its massive size (80,000 respondents from businesses across the world), remains the best kept secret of motivation. There was one question on the survey that, if staff ticked it, seemed to tally with high motivation: 'My supervisor cares about me'.[9] So, it seems there is indeed a silver motivational bullet. If you can tick 'yes' to this statement, the chances are you will be feeling good as you enter your school.

---

9 See http://www.gallup.com/businessjournal/493/item-supervisor-cares-about.aspx.

Boom. That's it. We can't prove this but we strongly suspect that the same principle applies to the children at school. If those in your charge can tick yes to: 'Someone at school seems to care about me as a person', then their odds of feeling motivated are good. Let that person be you.

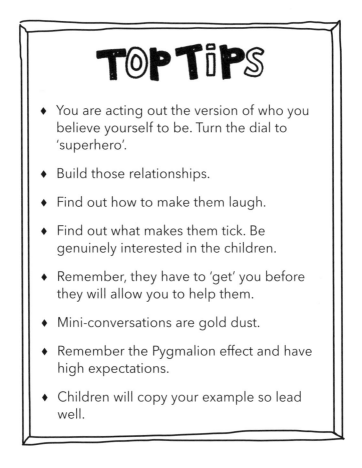

TOP TiPS

- You are acting out the version of who you believe yourself to be. Turn the dial to 'superhero'.

- Build those relationships.

- Find out how to make them laugh.

- Find out what makes them tick. Be genuinely interested in the children.

- Remember, they have to 'get' you before they will allow you to help them.

- Mini-conversations are gold dust.

- Remember the Pygmalion effect and have high expectations.

- Children will copy your example so lead well.

Lesson 4
MUCH MORE THAN SYLLABUS

'Thank you' is a limb worth going out on.

Schools are mad keen on measuring stuff and these measurements give data, which we can look at and which will help us do things faster and better. But it's our belief that the majority of the most important things in a school can't really be quantified. Try measuring creativity, excitement, commitment, buzz, happiness, confidence, team spirit or love. We'd argue that in a school, as in a business or family, it's the things that can't be counted that count the most.

There is a worldwide trend for the present generation of children to be more troubled emotionally than the last.[1] That's more angry, lonely, unruly, nervous and depressed. Childhood depression, once virtually unknown (or at least unrecognised), is emerging as commonplace. Among Americans born before 1905, the rate of major depression was 1%. For those born today it's 25%.[2] Cut to the UK and a recent Children's Society report revealed British children to be fourteenth out of fifteen in the international happiness league tables.[3] Our children are out-happied by those in Ethiopia and Algeria and while we're sure they're fabulous countries, come on, what the heck is going on?

We doubt it will surprise you to know that the early years are crucial in laying down our emotional landscape. Michael Meaney has a raft of eye-opening data, suggesting that the brain is shaped at a very early age and these early

---

1 Myrna M. Weissman, Priya Wickramaratne, Steven Greenwald et al., The Changing Rate of Major Depression: Cross-National Comparisons, *Journal of the American Medical Association* 268 (21) (1992): 3098–3105.

2 Peter M. Lewinsohn, Paul Rohde, John R. Seeley and Scott A. Fischer, Age Cohort Changes in the Lifetime Occurrence of Depression and Other Mental Disorders, *Journal of Abnormal Psychology* 102 (1993): 110-120.

3 Children's Society, *Good Childhood Report 2015* (London: Children's Society, 2015). Available at: http://www. childrenssociety.org.uk/what-we-do/resources-and-publications/the-good-childhood-report-2015.

experiences can change our chemistry and future behaviour.[4] He studied rats and found that the affectionate licking of rat pups actually determines how their brain chemicals respond to stress and that these patterns will be made in the ratlet's brain for life. Mums who were attentive and nurturing gave rise to a generation that were more quick witted and confident. Also, rather tellingly, the amount of love that the baby rat receives affects the amount of licking that the baby does to its own offspring in due course.

In very simple terms, a child's brain experiences crazy growth up to the age of 2. Everything is new to a 2-year-old and their brain soaks it up. It slackens off a wee bit after that but up until the age of 7 the brain is still buzzing with new learning. Imagine all the new neural pathways being laid down, creating branches through the brain. Your kids can learn anything. After 7 the branches start to get a severe pruning. If the neural pathways have been laid down but not used, they will be lopped off. Your brain detects that you haven't used them, so assumes you don't need them and, *snip snip*, those pathways are gone forever. This is also happening to children's social neurological branches. You might

---

4 Michael J. Meaney, Maternal Care, Gene Expression, and the Transmission of Individual Differences in Stress Reactivity Across Generations, *Annual Review of Neuroscience* 24 (2001): 1161–1192.

be looking after children who, through absolutely no fault of their own, have failings because their social connections haven't been used, and so were literally chopped off.

It's a very sad fact that some of the children in today's world have experienced very little affection. Nobody is going to read them a bedtime story or ask them what they've learned at school. It breaks our hearts when we hear about children turning up at primary school with very limited language. They can hardly speak, simply because they are living in a household where very little is said.

Andy once heard a man asking his lady friend, 'Why are you speaking to the baby. It can't even speak back?' and he shuddered. You might be astounded or slightly shocked by his sentence, but once the thought settles, you're probably not surprised.

We don't want to lay this on too heavily but, for some children, you will be the only positive person they interact with and your classroom their only loving environment. This not only creates a lump in our collective throats, it also raises the stakes about what you do on a daily basis.

Thinking inside the box

In order to be a more alive version of me, I had to drink from the cup of enthusiasm and risk people thinking I was bonkers or annoying. The alternative was to become a norm, a drone, whose life's purpose was only to remain within the accepted parameters of ordinariness. Rather than take a quick sip, I decided to drink deeply - *glug glug* - and accept the highs and the lows as a price worth paying for a life worth living.

Anon.

A child's readiness for school depends less on what they already know and more on whether they have figured out how to learn. An American study reports that there are seven key ingredients: confidence, curiosity, intentionality (the wish and capacity to have an impact), self-control, relatedness, capacity to communicate and cooperativeness.[5]

---

5 T. Berry Brazelton, *Heart Start: The Emotional Foundations of School Readiness* (Arlington, VA: National Center for Clinical Infant Programs, 1992).

Once again, without being too dramatic, this leads us to suggest that your role is not necessarily about teaching maths or English. These important subject skills pale into insignificance next to the seven essential learning skills outlined above. You are a role model. Model yourself well because your first job is to get the children ready for learning.

We've heard the phrase 'exam factories' and there's an element of truth in the fact that inspection pressures have ratcheted things up to a point where the syllabus is king. SATs scores in primary school and A*-C grades in secondary – that's the focus. But we all know this is only part of the picture. Tracking back, it was Howard Gardner's *Frames of Mind*[6] that gave an

---

6 Howard Gardner, *Frames of Mind: The Theory of Multiple Intelligences* (New York: Basic Books, 1993).

influential nudge to the first domino that began to topple the idea that IQ was the be-all-and-end-all of intelligence. Here's an example from Andy.

One of my best buddies, Pat, left school with no qualifications whatsoever. Zilch. I mean, after fifteen years of schooling, leaving empty handed is pretty much an achievement in its own right. (Yes, these were those 'good old days' that we keep harping back to. The days when Pat was allowed to slip under the radar and nobody actually noticed or, even worse, cared.) But my not-so-bright mate is now a fantastic dad who also runs a successful building company, and he can build houses, fit kitchens, plaster walls, lay patios and tile roofs. Meanwhile, I went on to get a PhD so must be 'proper clever', right? Er, wrong. If you ask me to put up a shelf, I guarantee it won't stay up for very long. And as for building a house or fitting a kitchen …

So, which of the two is the cleverest? Gardner's rather neat answer is both of them. He asserts that there are at least seven intelligences, only two of which – verbal and mathematical – are academic. Into the mix he tossed spatial (as in artists or architects), kinaesthetic (as in sport), musical (as in Mozart and Elvis) and a couple of

'personal intelligences' – interpersonal and intrapersonal. It is the combination of these so-called 'multiple intelligences' that makes up our all-round cleverness. Gardner, to his credit, said this was the starting point and that there was no magic number – later getting a bit too clever and stretching to a bewildering twenty intelligences.

But it's these last two personal intelligences that are of particular interest for this book. Gardner summarises them as follows: 'Interpersonal intelligence is the ability to understand other people: what motivates them, how they work, how to work cooperatively with them.' Or, stated in a slightly different way, 'Capacities to discern and respond appropriately to the moods, temperaments, motivations and desires of other people.'[7]

Intrapersonal intelligence is subtly but importantly different and is defined as 'a correlative ability, turned inward. It is a capacity to form an accurate model of oneself and to be able to use that model to operate effectively in life.' Or, with a slightly different spin, 'access to one's own feelings and the ability to discriminate among them and draw upon them to guide behaviour'.[8]

---

7 Howard Gardner, *Multiple Intelligences: The Theory in Practice* (New York: Basic Books, 1993), pp. 7, 9.
8 Gardner, *Multiple Intelligences*, pp. 7, 9.

In essence, we think you need to hone your interpersonal and intrapersonal intelligence in order to create a strong relationship with your learners. Plus, if you begin to think of intelligence as something much more than 'intellect', you will begin to recognise that you are assisting in bringing out a whole mixture of spatial, musical, sporting and social skills.

Think of it this way: everyone in school, whatever their role, is a teacher of literacy. The most common teaching method for spelling over the last two or three decades has been the look, cover, write, check method. But it doesn't work for everyone. Gary remembers one intelligent girl who had passed through the system up until Year 6 labelled a poor speller. She was great at art, though, and could model stuff and make things with ease. Gary gave her some modelling clay and taught her how to make letters and then move them into the positions to form words. He made a set of card letters out of cereal packets and gave them, with sticky tack, to her mother and showed her how to get her daughter to make words by moving the letters. He encouraged the girl to draw the words in her yard in the chalk he gave her and to paint them with water on hot days. It switched her on. She's now got a degree and is teaching English.

So, one of the things you must do is to consider how you help your learners. Are they better served by stomping and chanting those key words? Could they make the order of the planets into a rap? Or kick a football while talking about the key features of the Roman Empire?

The art of being a brilliant classroom assistant relies heavily upon planning.

Once you understand this, the art of being a brilliant classroom assistant relies heavily upon planning. It's unlikely that you will tap in to a child's true range of intelligences without spending some time thinking things through. This is easier said than done, especially in a secondary school where you have just been in PE and now you are in Spanish and you haven't seen that teacher for three days. However, the gold standard of being a great classroom

assistant tells us that effective planning between teacher and classroom assistant is essential. This should cover certain key areas:

♦ Which child (or children) are you there to support?

♦ What are their needs?

♦ Do they have a SEND statement?

♦ What is today's lesson about?

♦ What exactly do you want me to do?

The very best examples of good practice show that not only have the teacher and classroom assistant got their heads together before the lesson, but there is a process for the classroom assistant to feed back to the teacher both during and after the lesson. This enables them both to plan the next stage in the learning. We think this is the bit that makes the difference between someone who makes it up as they go along and someone who is part of a high performance learning team. Or, if you prefer, the difference between an amateur and professional classroom assistant.

The development of the SEND code of practice has refined our understanding of the role we can expect classroom assistants to play. Some teachers had become used to requesting 'support' in class for dealing with challenging kids,

but the shift towards individual learning needs gives us a much narrower definition of the role, concentrating more closely on young people with clearly identified and defined requirements. This focuses the job much more on working with individual kids rather than simply being there to assist with classroom management or to provide a comfort blanket to teachers when there are difficult pupils in the class.

It also places more emphasis on working with small groups of young people to enable their learning to progress. For classroom assistants, this provides us with a key performance indicator: your presence must be seen to have an impact on progress in learning. It is no longer enough to be there to hand out pencils and calm a child who is off task – you are required to have an impact on learning.

So let's share a top tip before we reach the end of this chapter. In fact, two top tips, coined by Dale Carnegie in his epic 1936 book, *How to Win Friends and Influence People*.[9] First, be *genuinely* interested in the children. The trick is to be less interested in yourself and more interested in them or, to use slightly clunky language, it's an equal split of 'self-esteem' and 'us-esteem'.

---

9 Dale Carnegie, *How to Win Friends and Influence People* (New York: Simon & Schuster, 1936).

Second, here's another corker that still holds true today: say nice things about the kids and teacher behind their backs. It's likely that the grapevine will whisper it back to them, and how morale boosting is it to hear that someone is saying nice things about you when you're not even there? The blue touchpaper of a relationship is lit. You will also have indulged in something called 'spontaneous trait transference' which basically means that if you are saying nice things about someone, the person to whom you're saying nice things attributes those qualities to you. This is all done at a subconscious level, but we promise you that makes it more powerful rather than less.

Another corker!

TOP TIPS

- Converse with the children using positive language. You should aim to become a non-shouty role model.

- Think of your role as wider than the curriculum. You are there to draw out intelligence in all its forms.

- Hone your own social intelligence skills in order to create rapport.

- Plan. (Try the 7 Ps: Prior Preparation and Planning Prevents Piss Poor Performance.)

- Work with the teacher at the planning stage. In fact, insist on this.

- Be genuinely interested in the children.

- Say nice things about them behind their backs and let the grapevine whisper it back to them.

- Consider what sort of learner they are and tailor your input to match their learning style.

Lesson 5
RULES, PROCEDURES AND SERIOUS STUFF

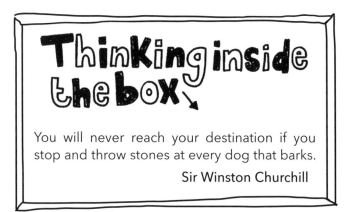

Thinking inside the box

You will never reach your destination if you stop and throw stones at every dog that barks.

Sir Winston Churchill

Gowned professors with brains like supercomputers have delved deep into the reasons for educational underachievement and have come up with profound analyses of the causes, but we were intrigued by a rather more down-to-earth theory which puts forward the contention that it is all down to dining tables.

Let us explain. Allegedly 50% of homes in the UK do not now have a dining table. What do you do at a dining table? Well, yes, of course, you eat. But you also talk, you converse, you exchange ideas and you build up those language skills that are the baseline of achievement. What's more is that you learn to discuss rather than argue, debate rather than fall out and, if you play it correctly, share the highlight of your day.

The average number of internet-enabled devices in every UK home is now 7.4.[1]

When it comes to selecting holiday reading, school policies are probably not right up there competing with a bestseller from Waterstones. Indeed, the mere mention of 'school policies' can send a chill through your bones, yet they remain the essential bedrock of a school

---

1 See http://www.theguardian.com/technology/2015/apr/09/online-all-the-time-average-british-household-owns-74-internet-devices.

community. They bind everyone together in common endeavour and, most importantly, they are there to protect us when things go wrong. They inform us about the procedures and systems the school has in place, but they also underpin the very core purpose of the school: to provide the best education possible to enable as many young people as possible to achieve their full potential.

So let's start with the literacy policy. There is a common assumption that literacy is solely concerned with the written word, but in fact it is concerned with all forms of communication. Teachers may refer to 'oracy' but what we really mean is talking. The best classroom assistants do this very well. Let's have a closer look.

Brilliant classroom assistants use every opportunity to talk with the children, to get them to articulate their understanding and to probe

what they are learning. Talking will lead to learning. It can often seem so much easier just to tell a child the answer, but this is a short term sticking plaster. It does not allow learning to progress. Great classroom assistants use starters like, 'Tell me …', or 'Why …?' or 'How …?' All of these questions require kids to develop their language skills and therefore their understanding.

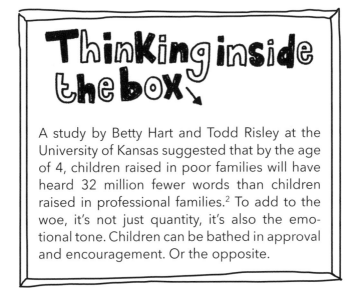

Thinking inside the box

A study by Betty Hart and Todd Risley at the University of Kansas suggested that by the age of 4, children raised in poor families will have heard 32 million fewer words than children raised in professional families.[2] To add to the woe, it's not just quantity, it's also the emotional tone. Children can be bathed in approval and encouragement. Or the opposite.

2   Betty Hart and Todd R. Risley, The Early Catastrophe: The 30 Million Word Gap by Age 3, *American Educator*, Spring (2003): 4-9.

We watched a great Year 7 lesson on volcanoes recently in which the teacher presented the information about the structure of volcanoes via a shrewd variety of media before setting up a card sorting activity. The classroom assistant, who was working with pupils Joseph and Mionie, constantly encouraged them to think aloud as they sorted their cards, with questioning along the lines of, 'Mionie, tell me, how many parts of the volcano can you remember? How many could you see from two miles away? Why would it be dangerous to go closer? Tell me what happens when the volcano starts to erupt ...' She was particularly clever in disguising what she was doing by saying things like, 'I didn't know anything about volcanoes. I didn't quite get the bit about ...' This turned the tables and made the child do the teaching, which is a brilliant way of consolidating learning.

In answer to the last one, it was interesting that Joseph started by making erupting noises, but the classroom assistant persisted and encouraged him to find words to describe the process, and he started to come up with words like 'rumble', 'crash' and 'explode'. She also coaxed Mionie to recognise that they were verbs. The classroom assistant had whiteboards, one each for Joseph, Mionie and herself. Each person wrote down the words they were using, which enabled the two children to see the spellings of these words so they could use them

successfully later in the lesson. She also had a prompt sheet with an outline of a volcano into which she had written some sentence starters she had agreed with the teacher to support their writing. This was all great work to support literacy and all were strategies in the school's literacy policy.

The real secret of this masterclass in being a brilliant classroom assistant is that she achieved it without distracting from the teacher. There is nothing more difficult for a teacher leading a lesson than to have a classroom assistant talking to the learners they are there to support and having to talk over them. It makes it doubly hard work for the teacher and distracts other children as well. Timing is everything.

Schools will store their policies in different places. They could be in a staff handbook in paper form, on the school network or virtual learning environment or online. Wherever they are tucked away, it is worth your weight in gold to search them out. Most schools will have a plethora of them and some will not naturally jump off the page or the screen at you.

We would suggest every classroom assistant reads and absorbs the school's behaviour policy. It is almost certainly going to explain in some detail what the expectations are for behaviour, how to respond to inappropriate behaviour and, critically, how to encourage

good behaviour. Typically it will include sanctions and rewards. The best classroom assistants know not only what the procedures are for dealing with incidents but they also have a clear agreement with the teacher as to who does what. If a kid misbehaves, where are the demarcation lines between what the classroom assistant would be expected to do and the point at which the teacher takes control? If there is an incident to record on the school system, who is going to do it? Who will administer a punishment, such as a detention?

Behaviour policies will also include information about the school's reward systems. We are going to look further at the power of praise and how to give it in another chapter (see Lesson 7), but for now let's content ourselves by acknowledging the importance of pre-empting bad behaviour by building positive relationships with children, starting with the most reluctant. They are the ones to get in your pocket as soon as possible. Using every available strategy for rewarding good behaviour will be a hugely influential motivator for learning, which in turn means you will have fewer incidents to deal with that require punishment.

Celebrate what you want to see more of.

Tom Peters

There will be other policies stashed away fairly close to the overall behaviour policy which merit close attention as well – for example, the uniform policy. It doesn't matter how long you have been in a school, much as you may feel that you have a firm grasp on what the expectations are, there are always grey areas where you find yourself in a sea of uncertainty. Are they allowed to wear hoodies inside? Are they allowed two earrings? Are pumps acceptable footwear? Is make-up allowed?

This matters for three reasons at least. First, young people will test you out, and if they know that you haven't picked them up for doing something wrong, they will have you down as a soft touch and will respect you less. Second, it is always embarrassing when the deputy head walks in and reprimands a child for having their tie undone or wearing a hat when you have

been sitting next to them for a whole morning. It doesn't reflect well on you. Third, it makes life difficult for another colleague when they challenge the child later in the day, only to get the riposte, 'Mr Snidgepodge didn't say anything about it this morning.'

Mobile phones will be another area where it is critical that you know what to do. Some schools allow their use, others do not. Most will insist that they are switched off in class or at least on silent. What should you do if a child contravenes this rule? Have you agreed with the teacher how to deal with this? It is vital that you know because young people are understandably very protective of their phones. They are expensive bits of kit and they are usually very proud of their latest acquisition. If your inclination is that it is appropriate to confiscate the phone, you need to be sure what your school policy says on the matter.

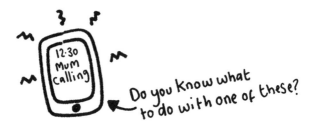

Bullying is another area to familiarise yourself with, and your school will certainly have a policy on this. It may be integrated into the overall behaviour policy or it may stand on its own. Because of the media attention on bullying, it is often a trigger reaction from kids to say that they are being bullied, when in actual fact they have simply fallen out. As a classroom assistant, it is essential that you know what bullying is and how to deal with it. Where genuine bullying occurs, it can have the most extraordinarily negative effect on a child, and it often stays under the radar, so it's crucial to be sharp on this. Bullying is a calculated, deliberate intention to be cruel, unpleasant or unkind which is repeated over a period of time. It can be physical or verbal, or sometimes it can simply result from the look, the glare or the stare. Bullies often hunt in packs and they pick on children they perceive to be weaker.

We have learned over the years never to proclaim proudly that we work in a school where there is no bullying. We deal with it rigorously, certainly, but to say there is no bullying would be an illusion. When the bullying is in the open and obvious it can be dealt with, but much bullying is covert and takes place away from the eyes and ears of staff. Classroom assistants are in pole position to pick up vibes on this. As they work with individual kids, snippets of information tend to come out about what is going on in

dark corners. PE changing rooms, the school bus, dinner queues and toilets are favourite haunts of the bully.

Here's a tale of two children and two classroom assistants. Frank was an unusual boy. He was in every way a bit different to most of the other lads. Charlie was the opposite and definitely cool. At lunchtimes he was a key player on the yard, or so it seemed. Frank was into reading about superheroes and would read one of his books as soon as he arrived in every class until the teacher asked him to put it away. He would often pretend to be asleep in lessons. Sometimes he would deliberately annoy the others by making weird noises. Charlie was always at the centre of a football game, whether it was played with a sponge ball or a bottle. Whenever the class were asked to get into groups or pairs, Frank was always left out. The classroom assistant who worked with Frank's class in art discovered that he was followed home every night by a group of older boys. He tried different routes but it still happened. They would often push and shove him, but he was scared to say anything because he was frightened of 'snitching'. Frank had put up with this for weeks but it took a random comment to the classroom assistant to enable the school to put measures in place to help him and the daily threatening he was suffering from those older boys stopped. Similarly, on noticing that Charlie was very

agitated when he came in from lunchtime to his next lesson, the classroom assistant assigned to a mate of his asked if he was alright. Charlie's story, which wasn't as obvious, then came out too. Despite all his outward appearances of being a confident young lad, he poured his heart out that he was being bullied day in, day out by a small group of other boys who regularly intruded on his game and wrecked it. The school was then able to help Charlie too.

Classroom assistants are in the front line when it comes to kids confiding in them about their troubles, so it is essential that they are familiar with the school's safeguarding policy. It's clear why we need to be sharp in this area, so while we have no need to explain the historical origins of such a need, it can cause much angst. Even for those who are imbued with a positive outlook on life and a natural disposition to think that other human beings are decent and wholesome, it is shocking to read on an almost daily basis of the sickening abuse of children.

For every single person who works in a school, their one paramount responsibility is to safeguard the health and well-being of the children in their care. We have alluded already to the steps that will be taken by the school to ensure safe recruitment of staff (see Lesson 1). Classroom assistants, by definition, will be working with some vulnerable children, often on a

one-to-one basis. They are an indispensable part of the antennae which will pick up signs that all may not be well.

Abuse in all its horror comes in many different shapes and forms, and these will be explained in the school's safeguarding policy. In fact, your school should provide training to everyone yearly on that policy. In some senses, physical abuse is the most obvious to detect, and class-room assistants who work with children while they are getting changed for PE have a crucial role to play. They may see bruises and marks which will give rise to concern and need further investigation. Emotional abuse is more obscure but classroom assistants who work individually with kids may be the first to notice changes in behaviour or pick up information in the course of classroom conversation. Sexual abuse can often be kept under wraps, but again it is during normal classroom interaction that things are sometimes divulged which may ring alarm bells. Neglect is perhaps more apparent – classroom assistants are very observant when it comes to a child who is dirty, smelly or hungry.

The safeguarding policy will give clear guid-ance on what to do in all of these cases, and it will cover other areas as well. In a nutshell, the appropriate response is never to sit on the information. Never agree to keep a secret. Always tell someone else and make a record

which you sign and date with a note of what you know. Find out who your safeguarding officer (or designated safeguarding person (DSP)) is in school and follow the procedures in the school policy.

The policy for special educational needs and disability is very important to your role. Clearly, classroom assistants will be working with learners who have a wide range of needs. The recently revised code of practice for SEND makes the definition of exactly what this classification constitutes much tighter, which means that alongside those who are identified on school systems, there will be many others for whom learning is difficult for one reason or another and who will also need additional intervention.

Those who are officially recognised as having a particular learning or physical need will have an education, health and care plan (EHCP). This is a detailed document with a description of the child's difficulties and a planned programme for that child. It is absolutely essential that classroom assistants who work with these children have read and absorbed this document. Obviously it will help them to meet the child's requirements, but there are also regular review and reporting back procedures in place and the classroom assistant may be asked to contribute to these.

There will be other young people who you will come into contact with, bringing with them a wide range of sometimes complex needs. Again, a brilliant classroom assistant will take time to find out as much information as possible about these kids. This will almost certainly mean that you will encounter children who have significant difficulties with reading and writing, some of whom (but by no means all) will come under the banner headline of 'dyslexic'. There will also be learners who have attention deficit hyperactivity disorder (ADHD) or who are on the autistic spectrum.

All of these terms may be overwhelming for a new classroom assistant, so it is well worth the investment of effort in spending designated time with the SEND team to gain an understanding of what is involved – in particular, how best to help kids who are not confident readers or spellers. There are very specific strategies which you can employ to help develop the skills of these students in such a way that you complement the work being done by teachers, and it is worth asking for training to do this.

Finally on policies, brilliant classroom assistants take time to read and understand the terms and conditions of employment with regard to their job. Classroom assistants are employed under different contracts to teachers. Hours will be specified and there may be different

arrangements for signing in and out, asking for leave and procedures to follow in case of sickness, so make sure you are up to speed with the conventions at your school.

Policies and procedures aren't the most thrilling documents, so this perhaps hasn't been the most page-turning chapter. But in the job that you do, it absolutely pays to be on the ball, hence our refresher.

It absolutely pays to be on the ball!

TOP TiPS

- We are all teachers of literacy.

- Talk with children. Remember some of them hear very little positive language at home.

- Get them to talk with you.

- Read your school's behaviour policy. Know what to do if a situation escalates.

- Make sure you know the deal on uniform and mobile phones.

- Be up to speed on how to respond to bullying.

- Safeguarding: this should be at the top of your agenda every day.

- Read the SEND policy and find out as much as you can.

OUTSTANDING

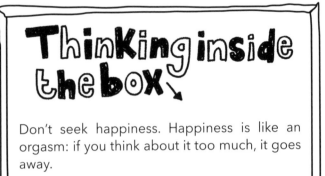

Thinking inside the box

Don't seek happiness. Happiness is like an orgasm: if you think about it too much, it goes away.

Tim Minchin

At the beginning of the book we made a serious pitch for the role of classroom assistant being considered a career, not just a job. We also put our hearts on our sleeves to proclaim that an awesome classroom assistant is priceless. We have seen the results on a daily basis, and there are some tricks of the trade that we have noticed from the very best

← Our hearts on our sleeves

practitioners which we think are worth passing on.

First up, we want you to fit in, but only just. You need to pitch in at the upper end of whatever is acceptable in your school. Have a look around and be determined to be up there with the best. That means you're the smartest, the smiliest and the most upbeat. Not so smiley that you terrify people, but enough to stand out for the right reasons!

Be the BEST

Be the Smiliest

Be the Smartest

Stand out for right reasons

Be most upbeat
#The BESTclassroomassistantintheworld

Like all those who work with young people in schools, classroom assistants are constant role models. This has implications for the way they personally present themselves. There is therefore a requirement to adopt a professional dress code. This will vary from school to school with some insisting on a formal professional image, while others are a bit more relaxed. The trick is to make sure that you are in tune with the expectations of your establishment.

There is a qualification here because of the practical nature of the role. Some classroom assistants – for example, in special schools – will often work on a soft floor mat helping children to explore and learn, while classroom assistants in certain practical subjects will want to wear clothing which is appropriate for what could be a messy activity. Common sense should prevail, but the young classroom assistant in a quite formal secondary who did not arrive at school in a shirt and tie was missing a trick. The kids immediately knew he wasn't a teacher and, in turn, accorded him less respect. Many schools work on the principle of 'look smart, think smart', so make sure you are on the same wavelength.

On a similar tack, find out what the school rules are and go with them. One school we visited recently had a very firm line on mobile phones in school, and we saw no evidence of their use

in school by students. We are not naive enough to believe that the kids didn't have them in their bags, but we were unsettled to see a classroom assistant, new to the school, in the playground clearly making a phone call. It wasn't a great example or a great start.

In a different school there was a clear expectation that children did not take food out of the dining room to minimise problems with litter. It was surprising therefore to see an adult taking food outside and we noticed a group of likely lads seizing on the opportunity to point this out to the supervisory staff. The message is clear: classroom assistants are bound by the rules of the establishment just as much as teachers.

Allow us to expand briefly on this for a moment. A school we know undertook a review of its behaviour policy recently and took advice from well-known gurus on the subject at a London based workshop. One of the messages which came over loud and clear was that there is a massive correlation between the behaviour of the adults and the behaviour of the children. The message went out to every member of staff: behave as you want the kids to behave. We have witnessed many an occasion when a member of staff has been telling a child off for lack of respect and poor manners, when frankly the manner in which the adult was talking

showed absolutely no respect to the young person at all. Not surprising then if the child comes back at them.

It is also worth thinking about how you and the teacher will address each other. For reasons which we have never quite been able to fathom, it is always a source of endless fascination for kids to know the first names of their teachers. It may be that it's the culture of your school for students to use first names, but where the norm is for adults to be addressed as Mrs, Miss, Mr or Sir, remember not to slip into Michelle or Deirdre (especially if their names are Keith and Bob) in front of the kids.

Classroom assistant: yes, it's a tricky term. Who exactly are they assisting? Is it the kids, or is it the teacher? We could take a tangent here and explore the relative merits of each but that would be to miss the point. The function is actually dual and complementary. A classroom assistant assists the teacher in helping the kids to learn. This has implications for the classroom assistant – and we have witnessed some of our colleagues get this wrong and come unstuck.

You are at all times a member of staff. We have seen classroom assistants who have got too close to the kids and have ended up getting involved in gossip and inappropriate conversations. When you are working alongside a child for an extended period of time, it is natural that

you form a close bond. But remember that it's a professional bond with clear limits. We heard of a young female classroom assistant who had been working alongside some Year 9 boys. The conversation turned to cars and she happened to have a soft top Mini which had been noticed by the lads. After school the assistant head found her sitting in the car with the boys so they could admire its specifications. No harm was intended but it was not appropriate.

Similarly, if you live locally and know certain families, or have a child or relative in the school, you have to make sure that you and they know how to behave in school. It isn't appropriate for a child to call you 'Uncle John' or for your son to see you every breaktime for a bit of reassurance. That's what the school pastoral system is for.

In the same way, there will be topics of conversation which are unsuitable. A young Spanish classroom assistant found the discussion running away with him as his teenage audience started to make hay on the subject of swear words in Spanish. It's also worth noting that politics and personal viewpoints are best left at the school gate. However, we did enjoy the Year 11 child who came to us during a recent election and said that one of the classroom assistants had voted for a party which wasn't exactly, shall we say, mainstream. He went on to clarify: 'She

will remain nameless … because I don't actually know her name.' Classic. Of course, this does not mean that politics cannot be discussed. Far from it; it simply means that you are well advised not to share your own point of view while you probe their understanding of the issues.

An area where classroom assistants can get inadvertently drawn in is discussion about teachers or colleagues. Kids are sometimes very ready to give their opinions about members of staff, but this is where clear lines of confidentiality, professionalism and neutrality must prevail. Brilliant classroom assistants do not allow themselves to be drawn in, or take any action, unless they feel it is a safeguarding issue or something unprofessional. In which case they would refer it on.

In some senses classroom assistants are in a very privileged position. You have a grandstand view of various teachers, especially in a secondary school, and you may see lessons where the teacher has found the going tough. It is absolutely essential for the relationship between teachers and classroom assistants that they do not gossip or chit-chat about the performance of individual teachers. They should be on the same team sheet at all times and owe each other total loyalty.

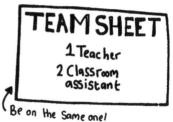

TEAM SHEET

1 Teacher

2 Classroom assistant

Be on the same one!

In terms of discretion and the observance of confidentiality, the same goes for the SEND records of individual children. We discussed earlier the education, health and care plans which are kept about kids who are formally on the SEND register, but there will be a welter of other personal information about young people in circulation. This should remain strictly confidential in all circumstances.

We are not foolish enough to think that every school day is hunky-dory. We know that in a very high pressure environment, people's nerves get frayed and they want to sound off or make a point. There is an accepted place, time and way of doing this. One of the hallmarks of brilliant classroom assistants is they are an absolute pleasure to work with; however, it is not always the case. We can all think of colleagues who like the sound of their own voice, the barrack room lawyers who can whip up a storm of negativity in a trice, taking others with them. Even worse are those who write shouty emails – you know, the ones written in capital letters. This is not professional behaviour and brilliant classroom assistants do not do it. There is a time and a manner in which to air grievances, and having a public chunter is not one of them. Pause, breathe, think and then deal with the matter in a measured and calm way.

There is a rider to all of this. We mentioned that classroom assistants are often local to the school, whereas teachers often choose, for obvious reasons, to live a little removed from the school. This means that classroom assistants can be a vital organ of communication about the word on the street. Many a time we have discovered that the reason a child may be behaving erratically in school is because they are being allowed to run fast and loose in their social time. When talking to the parents of a child who is in danger of becoming wayward it can be very instructive to ask how things are at home, although often the answer is that things are fine. This can be thrown into sharper relief when your classroom assistant tells you that the child in question is frequently seen in the local park at the dead of night. Herein lies another way in which classroom assistants are invaluable to school life.

Finally, let's talk about the use of social media. If there is one thing we would choose to spirit away from our day-to-day lives, it would be the prevalence of social media that gets in the way of learning in schools. Time and again we have found ourselves in the middle of a frenzy of bile being exchanged between children, parents and their wider families. There are lessons to be learned for everyone who works in a school as

well. There will almost certainly be a policy for this in your school, so make sure you read it and take on board what it says.

Let us take things one by one. First phones. We find ourselves wondering what life was like before mobile phones, much as the Victorians presumably wondered what life was like before electricity. Astonishingly we survived. Now, if we leave the house without our phones we are bereft. The problem, of course, is that a phone is not just a phone. It will contain contacts, messages and probably photos, so make sure yours is safe at all times. We felt for the young female classroom assistant who left her phone on her desk with her keys, only to find that the nerdy kid in the front row had worked out her password and was looking with great relish at the pictures of her sunbathing topless on a sun-kissed beach in Malta. He then shared them on social media. She never returned to the school. She couldn't face the children again.

Second, social media sites. Ensure yours are locked down and that only friends can see your posts (all the different applications have this facility). What was a huge wheeze at the rugby club or the wedding reception in Mexico does not always look so clever if your kids, your colleagues or your head teacher get to see what you've been up to.

Still on social media sites, think carefully about what you are posting. The rule of thumb here is that what happens in school should remain in school. You will be well advised not to post photos of anything in school or discuss what happens in school. There needs to be a clear line delineating what is professional, and therefore confidential, from your personal life. We've had to deal with the consequences of colleagues tittle-tattling online when genuine upset has been caused, bemoaning all the time that it could so easily have been avoided.

The bottom line in all of this is that we rate classroom assistants very highly and we think you deserve the highest professional respect. Many classroom assistants come into the job without any formal training, so we think it's worthwhile to rehearse the prerequisites of working in a school so that you may enjoy the professional status you deserve. We want you to immerse

yourself in the school culture and create positive working relationships with the children, but be careful out there – it can be a minefield.

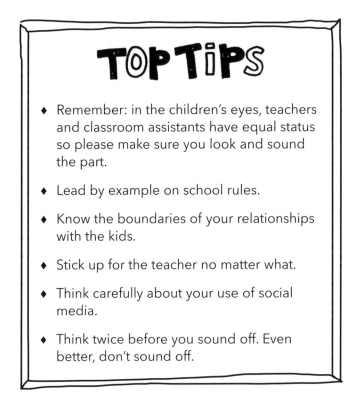

TOP TIPS

- Remember: in the children's eyes, teachers and classroom assistants have equal status so please make sure you look and sound the part.

- Lead by example on school rules.

- Know the boundaries of your relationships with the kids.

- Stick up for the teacher no matter what.

- Think carefully about your use of social media.

- Think twice before you sound off. Even better, don't sound off.

CHALLENGING KIDS

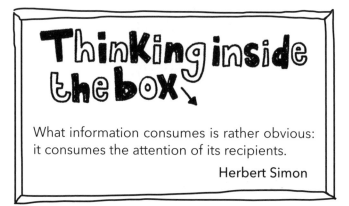

Thinking inside the box

What information consumes is rather obvious: it consumes the attention of its recipients.

Herbert Simon

It comes with the territory that you will work with some challenging young people. The children who find their journey through school pretty much plain sailing are not the ones who classroom assistants are typically employed to help. We know a classroom assistant who is heading for the (potentially) greener pastures of full teacher training. She bade farewell to her school and said all the usual things about how much she had enjoyed her time and thanked her colleagues in time honoured fashion, but she went on to reveal that there were times when she had

gone home in tears. Being a brilliant classroom assistant is no picnic – or, if it is, it's one where it rains a lot. You will find yourself in situations which will draw on every sinew and every nerve.

It's no picnic but it's so worth it

Thinking inside the box

What price happiness? According to a researcher from the University of London's Institute of Education,[1] here are some monetary values of happiness:

♦ Having a fulfilling job is worth £40k a year.

1 Nattavudh Powdthavee, Putting a Price Tag on Friendships, Relatives, and Neighbours: Using Surveys of Life Satisfaction to Value Social Relationships, *The Journal of Socio-economics* 37(4) (2008): 1459–1480. Available at: http://www.powdthavee.co.uk/resources/ valuing_social_relationships_15.04.pdf.

- Seeing friends and relatives is equivalent to a pay rise of £64k a year.

- Chatting to nice neighbours is worth £37k a year.

- Getting married is worth £50k a year.

And the biggy?

- Excellent health is estimated to be worth £300k a year.

We sincerely hope you can tick some of the boxes above. Of course, it's easy to pick holes or make cheap jibes (the researcher has clearly never met my wife, etc.). But the wider point about relationships and health is staggering. So here's a very big point: we are ingratitude spotters, fixating on all the stuff that we haven't yet got. We spend oodles of hard earned cash chasing trinkets.

Taking the argument to the extreme, you could trade in your fulfilling job, family, friends, neighbours and good health and collect £491,000. You'd be nearly half a million pounds richer but so much poorer.

One of the difficulties is that we are all predis-posed to see the negative at the expense of the positive. This comes as part of the 'human being' pre-programme, given at birth. Rather than go into detail as to why, let's just say that, for most people, it's easier to be negative. This is especially relevant when you've had a bad lesson or a bad day. Many a time we've heard teachers and classroom assistants say of the kids, 'They were horrendous today.'

Before you allow yourself to succumb to a vor-tex of despair, let us tease this one out. First, when things go wrong it is never personal. It may feel like it but it isn't. Almost certainly there is more going on than meets the eye. Being in a classroom with a group of children can be a very isolating experience, so when things don't work out we tend to think it's just us. But it doesn't usually take long in the course of staffroom conversation with other colleagues to discover that this child, or group of children, who has been so difficult has not reserved their mischievousness and awkwardness uniquely for you.

Nine times out of ten you will discover that there is other stuff going on. What else has been happening in the course of the school day? Have there been problems elsewhere? Has it been a wet lunchtime? Has something kicked off in the dining room? Has there been a

fall-out in the playground? Was there a difficulty in another lesson? Is there often a problem in this particular session? What about outside of school? Has something happened on a social media site? Is something going on at home? Are there friendship issues? First base is to see if you can find out what the backstory might be.

As a child, Zaphod had been diagnosed with ADHDDAAADHD (ntm) ABT which stood for Always Dreaming His Dopey Days Away, Also Attention Deficit Hyperflatulence Disorder (not to mention) A Bit Thick.

Eoin Colfer in Douglas Adams's,
The Hitchhiker's Guide to the Galaxy

So before you crucify yourself with angst about how awful the situation was, stop your mind from running away with you. When you say 'horrendous', do you actually mean wall-to-wall horrendous? When you start to unpick what went wrong, you usually arrive at a situation where you are saying, 'Well, he wasn't horrible *all* lesson. In fact, he did the first activity really well, and he was okay with the bit when they had to get into groups. He lost it when ...' In this way you can start to get a bit of perspective on the situation.

Our best tip is to draw back from the fray and let your nerves settle. We all know how frustrating it can be when dealing with an awkward customer, for no better reason that it is an affront to our pride and it hurts when things go wrong. This is not the right state of mind in which to try to sort things out. Much better to take a deep breath, go away and come back fresh the next time. The danger is that when you are cross, and potentially the child is cross as well, you will end up making an already difficult situation worse.

Thinking inside the box

The common adage is that in order to calm down you step back and count to ten. However, scientists suggest that it takes approximately twenty minutes for your body to recover after an explosion of adrenaline, so we suggest you retreat to the staffroom, have a cuppa and count to 1,200.

Take 20 mins, a cuppa (maybe a biscuit for good measure) and CALM DOWN

Whenever you are dealing with an awkward child, you should have one thing in your mind and one thing only: next time you want better work and better behaviour. The game is to persuade them to engage in the learning. If you give full vent to your own personal frustrations, you will end up either with a child who is cussed and resentful or a child who has simply switched off.

Chris had an illuminating experience at a busy roundabout recently. He was en route to a training event and had to stop for petrol. On emerging back onto the roundabout, there was loud and ferocious hooting from his right. Exactly what the cause of the problem was he was not entirely certain but he suspected he was in the wrong lane. Looking in his mirror, a red faced angry man was berating Chris for his driving skills. Worse was to follow. The traffic lights which would allow him to escape this tirade were on red so he drew up alongside, still ranting. He would have made an excellent candidate for the role of pantomime villain. He tried to entice Chris to wind his window down so he could hear his vilification more clearly. Chris wasn't tempted to oblige and enjoyed the reprieve of a green light.

What does this show us? Once the man started shouting and screaming Chris just switched off. Remember that fight or flight stuff from

earlier: Chris's brain went into reptilian mode and was just searching for a way out. He wasn't going to listen while he was being berated. We might suggest the fuming motorist was having a bad hair day but he didn't have any. Chris was probably the victim of him being late, stressed, having a row with his partner, not earning enough that morning or all of the above.

It's the same with the kids. There is often a back-story. Damien is a lad who had great difficulty being told off by teachers. After exclusions and multiple sanctions, it was discovered that Damien's parents had recently separated and that he had witnessed increasingly severe and often physical rows between them. He was deeply damaged psychologically and emotion-ally by this, and therefore whenever he was on the receiving end of tellings off and shouting, he either shut down or gave the teacher choice advice as to what to do next.

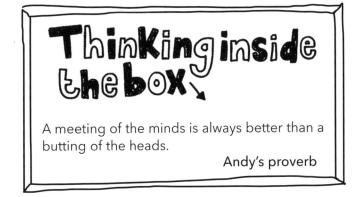

Thinking inside the box

A meeting of the minds is always better than a butting of the heads.

Andy's proverb

The way to achieve better work and better behaviour is by total positivity, no matter what. Always start afresh with a renewed commitment to that total positivity. Do not let us delude you: this can be immensely challenging. It might be hardwired into us to want our pound of flesh if someone has given us a hard time. But that will not lead you into the golden territory where you will achieve better work and better behaviour. Always treat the young person with respect. By discussing what went wrong in a calm and measured way, you have doubled your chances of gaining the esteem of the child in question and you have hugely increased your chances of reducing the likelihood of it happening again.

Another key tip to handling these situations is to make sure you have listened to their side of the story, and signposted this to them clearly. The biggest gripe difficult kids have about staff is that they 'don't listen'. This is not always strictly true but it is their perception, so make sure they know that you are giving them their chance to be heard. Always thank them at the end of every conversation.

We would like you to consider that many of the most challenging young people are likely to have grown up on a diet of criticism, and this often starts from the earliest days of their life. We have encountered hosts of challenging kids with whom we have worked tirelessly in school,

only to find that a mere weekend, let alone a summer holiday, undoes everything we have been trying to achieve because they return home to an environment where they are routinely shouted at and criticised. What we know about criticism is that it doesn't get results. It embeds negativity. Praise is the antidote.

The important point here is to know what to praise. It is no good issuing false praise. Praise must be genuine and it must be based on effort that results in progress. What you don't want are words of praise along the lines of, 'That is a superb drawing. You are so talented at this.' The problem with this type of comment is that it undermines the need to work hard. Why bother if you're talented? In his book, *Bounce*, Matthew Syed illustrates how praise linked to effort wins hands down when it comes to improvement and embedding an ability to tackle challenges.[2] We recommend that praise is not only focused on effort but is also linked to something they have done that has improved. This sort of praise is what you're after: 'That is a superb drawing. It shows what you can do with hard work and practice.' You need to be totally systematic about this. If you are working with a small group, make sure every child receives praise on a regular basis. You have to look for the stuff to

---

2 Matthew Syed, *Bounce: The Myth of Talent and the Power of Practice* (London: Fourth Estate, 2011).

praise them for – it may take a keen eye – but you can always find something they have done that represents progress.

Praise can also be a massive incentive. Let's say you have a reluctant homeworker. Rather than threaten them with a detention as a punishment, offer them a double gold star or merit as an incentive – if you can see they have put in a significant effort. Describe what you want to see so it's totally clear. Our experience shows this is more likely to secure the outcome you want. This can be backed up with a text or a tweet home. If your school has these technologies at its fingertips, do use them. They are immediate and go straight to the people who matter most: the folks at home. How brilliant for a child who does not always enjoy a lot of success at school to be greeted on their return home with, 'You've had a good day at school today, I hear. I got a text when I was in the supermarket by the frozen peas to say you were brilliant in English.' That's exactly what Gary did with Amanda, a student who hadn't really engaged in his class. After much persuasion she had made some progress and Gary sent a text home. The next day Amanda was back in, beaming and announcing

that her mum was so pleased she'd given her 'twenty quid'. Amanda's new effort meant she did really well in her English GCSE.

So, to finish, let us share the goal setting pyramid that was devised by the phenomenally motivating David Hyner. We find it an excellent way of getting the children to set a big goal and for them to work out, for themselves, what actions they need to take. We love Dave's pyramid because (a) it's simple and (b) it works. We advise that you use it at the start of each term, ideally on a one-to-one basis, to help get the students focused on their objectives.

Encourage them to come up with their goal, the bigger the better, and then, starting at the bottom of the pyramid, they work out what actions they need to take in order to get there. You make suggestions but the idea is that it is largely their work. Voilà, you have a clear hand-written representation of the actions they need to engage in.

How can we do better?

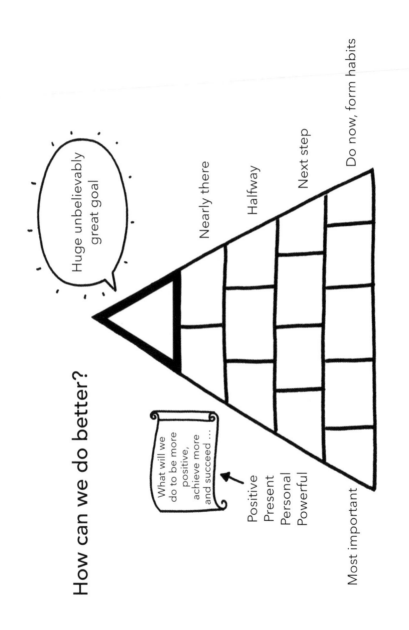

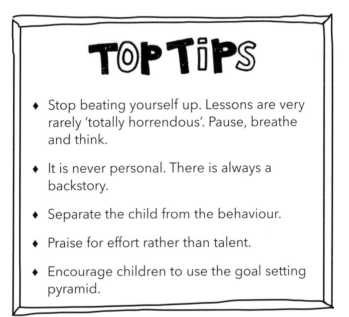

TOP TiPS

- Stop beating yourself up. Lessons are very rarely 'totally horrendous'. Pause, breathe and think.

- It is never personal. There is always a backstory.

- Separate the child from the behaviour.

- Praise for effort rather than talent.

- Encourage children to use the goal setting pyramid.

GIANT LEAPS OF LEARNING

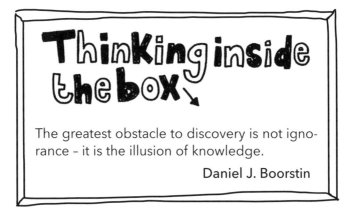

Thinking inside the box

The greatest obstacle to discovery is not ignorance - it is the illusion of knowledge.

Daniel J. Boorstin

Our experience suggests that there are three fundamental demands which children make of those who lead their learning: first that you are able to control them, second that you teach them something and, third, that they enjoy the learning – which is, perhaps, key to both.

The three fundamental demands

ENJOY the learning

control them

teach them

Curiously, however difficult they may make it for you and whatever obstacles they may throw in your way, they do *expect* to learn. Your best bet in dealing with awkward or challenging youngsters is therefore to teach them something. And, of course, it allows you to develop your relationship because you'll have something to praise them for when they've succeeded.

Here are some tips which will enable you to achieve some learning breakthroughs. We know that brilliant classroom assistants plan in advance with the teacher what the learning is going to be. When you are working with individual kids or groups of kids you have a chance to put your own spin on it to make the learning accessible to all. Right at the top of the list of helping children to learn is making sure they know how to learn and then giving them feedback as to how they have done and what they can do to improve further.

It's so easy to jump to assumptions. For example, do they know precisely what to do and how to do it? Grab yourself a pencil and in the frame on page 137, draw a house.

Now check the marking scheme at the end of the chapter and self-mark your work out of 10. Get any marks? We doubt it. And you're probably grumbling that it's not fair, in which case you're absolutely right! They key issue here is that we didn't tell you exactly what you'd pick

Grab one of these

Draw a house in here

up marks for, we didn't model it and we didn't show you exemplars or support you as you progressed. In the classroom, you'll need to do just that with your kids to signpost the learning for them. Planning with the teacher is crucial to your success in creating success for the children.

When you plan a lesson with the teacher you should have a precise idea of what the learning objective is for that lesson. Let us dwell for a moment on the difference between the 'doing' objective and the 'learning' objective. The answer to the question, 'What are they learning today?' is not 'cutting out shapes' or 'table tennis'. They might be learning how to use scissors to cut accurately or how to play a backhand, so make sure you are clear in your conversation with the teacher as to exactly what the children are learning.

Once you have that firmly established, brilliant classroom assistants customise the learning for their children. If you've picked up what we've been saying about relationships, you already know your learners well. You know what they're into – which TV programmes they watch, what's hot in sport for them, whether dance moves them, if they have favourite animals or are celebrity focused. Link this kid culture into the learning and you're going to have greater engagement. Link these things into starters

using key words, concepts and prior learning and you will further boost engagement and reinforce learning. Use props like cuddlies, customise worksheets with images, tweak tasks to incorporate their culture and they'll buy in even more. You'd be surprised how many Year 11s have been as motivated by a cuddly toy or a picture of the latest pop star as a Year 4 might be.

We came across a lovely quote recently: 'Do not train children to learn by force and harshness, but direct them to it by what amuses their minds, so that you may be better able to discover with accuracy the peculiar bent of the genius of each.' Music to the ears of every brilliant classroom assistant. Who said it? Plato. Nothing new there then. The more you interact with kids using activities they enjoy, the more they will learn, and therefore you will have made an impact on their progress.

Think back to what we said about different learning styles. We want children to remember what they are learning. Mix kid culture with what you know about their preferred learning style and again you've stepped up a gear. Here's a great example we witnessed in a Year 7 French class. The classroom assistant worked out mnemonics and rhymes for the numbers from 1 to 10 with two very challenging children along the lines of: what happened to 5 *Titanics*? Sank

(*cinq*). Did you have 8 Weetabix at breakfast? Wheat (*huit*). And so on – the learners were hooked. Similarly, in a special school the classroom assistant drew pictures which rhymed with the colours: a red bed, a purple turtle, a blue hair-do (we liked that one!).

What other magic ingredients are there which will help you, as a classroom assistant, to help them to learn? The obvious answer is to ask them. Never shirk from finding out from the kids themselves what helps them to learn. Do those word lists you always compile help them or confuse them? When you read together, does it always go on too long or do you cut it short just when they're getting into it? Ask them what helps them to learn and remember the virtue of listening to them. Seek out that kid culture. We call it broadcasting on Radio WiiiFM (What is in it For Me?).

Gone are the days when you could expect rows of docile children sitting and waiting to be told what to do and then doing it. The days of forcing learning down kids' throats like castor oil or syrup of figs is thankfully consigned to a gloomy and dusty place in the filing cabinet of educational history. Thank goodness. We want children to want to learn. What is in it for them may well be jobs and money and the best mobile phone. But simply wanting to learn is not always enough, as many of the young people you'll be working with don't think like that, especially the boys. They need a reason, so find one – real or spoof.

Younger children will go for totally imaginary scenarios. We recently saw a classroom assistant team up with the class teacher to dress up as Doctor Who and his assistant. The title music played and the TARDIS flew on the screen. They had only one hour to save the world by finding out what was the best diet for earthlings – and, boy, did they buy in. Throughout the lesson, both the doctor and his assistant regularly checked how the learning was going and corrected misconceptions. The morning was a joy-filled series of mini-plenaries wrapped in sci-fi packaging.

Getting the order of learning right is crucial in order to lead your students to it. One technique to try is to break it down into smaller parts – we

call this chunking. This is particularly useful for boys but it works well for both genders. The key is to take small learning steps where success can be celebrated and built on with the next step (or chunk). It's not TARDIS science – plenty of animals do it. Mother meerkats, for example, bring dead scorpions (a favourite food) to their young and encourage them to attack and devour them. Next she will bring live scorpions but with their sting removed, so they can repeatedly practise on them without any danger. Once she is certain they are proficient, she brings to them the real deal, so they can now use their skills to 'hunt' a fully functional scorpion.

The art of being brilliant with your students will rely on you completely understanding the learning the teacher wants to achieve in any given lesson or period of time. You will need to dissect that, discuss it with the teacher and break it into differentiated chunks that build the learning, meerkat style. We'll let you off standing on rocks to keep a lookout over the school though.

These are all ways of helping children to learn, which is the bread and butter of a brilliant classroom assistant. If it all seems a bit daunting, take your time. The likelihood is that you will be learning on the job, but some of the very best, most brilliant classroom assistants we have seen have done just that.

As we pointed out earlier, nobody ever said it was easy. Or fair. It's a tough job, but if it all seems too much, spare a thought for the commentator in the 100 metre race where Vasilis Papageorgopoulos and Jean-Louis Ravelomanantsoa were the leading contenders.[1] Now that was a difficult job.

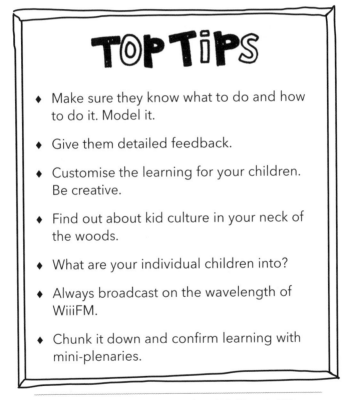

TOP TIPS

- ◆ Make sure they know what to do and how to do it. Model it.

- ◆ Give them detailed feedback.

- ◆ Customise the learning for your children. Be creative.

- ◆ Find out about kid culture in your neck of the woods.

- ◆ What are your individual children into?

- ◆ Always broadcast on the wavelength of WiiiFM.

- ◆ Chunk it down and confirm learning with mini-plenaries.

1 They were in the same heat in the 1972 Olympic 100 metre race.

House drawing marking scheme

★ Give yourself 10 out of 10 if yours looks anything like this!

Lesson 9

SMELLS LIKE TEAM SPIRIT

Thinking inside the box

Postcard from a negative member of staff:

Currently staying in Yosemite and it would be great but the mountains are blocking all the views.

A long serving colleague of ours took his leave from his school recently and the usual leaving speeches were made with due emotion on all sides, but one thing he said which struck a chord with us was when he talked about his future ambitions. He had lots of plans but, with a hint of sadness in his voice, he told his

attendant audience that, excited as he was about what lay ahead, the one thing he would miss was the company of his colleagues.

We have often compared working in a school with working in a hospital. Both are very specialised environments where daily life proceeds at a frenetic pace, with unforeseen events unfolding on a minute by minute basis. So, although there is a plan, there is also a great deal of thinking on your feet and reacting to circumstances as they arise. It's not quite 'making it up as you go along' but there will certainly be lessons where you feel like that.

←— you'll be thinking on these!

Thinking inside the box

When I was a young man, I wanted to change the world.

I found it was difficult to change the world, so I tried to change my nation.

When I found I couldn't change the nation, I began to focus on my town. I couldn't change the town and as an older man, I tried to change my family.

Now, as an old man, I realize the only thing I can change is myself, and suddenly I realize that if long ago I had changed myself, I could have made an impact on my family.

My family and I could have made an impact on our town.

Their impact could have changed the nation and I could indeed have changed the world.

Anon.

Teamwork is an essential ingredient in schools, particularly when your classroom is having one of those whirlwind days. Your interaction with your colleagues is therefore a pivotal part of your daily life. Now, we have discovered that there are colleagues and there are colleagues. There are colleagues with whom it is a pleasure to work, the sort who when you discover you have been put with them to measure the long jump pit on sports day, or on the same coach for the school trip, you find yourself looking forward to it. On the other hand, there are the ones

where you find your heart sinking when you find out you will be supervising the kids backstage with them for the Christmas show – because they are the professional moaners.

Nobody can doubt that working in a school is an intensively demanding task. Anyone who is hoping for an easy ride in life should apply else-where. Rewarding as it most certainly is, in our midst are colleagues who inhabit a twilight world of negativity in which there is always something to moan about. We call these peo-ple 'mood-hoovers' – you know, the sort of folk who will light up the staffroom *when they leave*. The trajectory of pessimism means there is always something to grumble about – from marking or a topic they don't want to teach to wet lunches or that new policy. It's a perpetual moaning machine. So the narrative goes on and on as it enters yet another spiral of doom and despair. Those who work in education can be their own worst enemies when it comes to heaping up their own misery. We refer to it as 'dinner plating' because it is like piling up the dirty dinner plates on the sideboard to be washed up. The pile gets higher and higher and the task becomes ever more insurmountable.

Classroom assistants have a clear choice to make in terms of their own personal and profes-sional behaviour. Andy has delved into the science of happiness to uncover the deep-seated psychology that explains why some people have a natural disposition towards the opposite of those colleagues described above – those who shine and radiate positivity in an infectious way. The solution is actually startlingly

straightforward. People who cheer us all up with their contagious good humour are not born like that; the midwife at the point of delivery does not instantly recognise a beatific smile which is a guarantor that this new little being will bring peace, happiness and sunshine into the world. They simply choose to be like that.

Andy describes this next point as a bit technical but very important. Your attitudinal choice is one of the biggest choices you can ever make, and yet it is one that is often missed. Choosing to be positive is common sense but by no means common practice. It is easier to make no choice at all, in which case the day will decide how you feel. In the hurly-burly of the classroom, the day will almost certainly drain you. But a few people have cottoned on to the fact that they can take charge of their lives, and they apply a modicum of effort into choosing to be upbeat and sparky. To be positive you have to work at it. The science suggests that it's simply easier to be negative, hence most people gravitate that way. But you don't have to be 'most people'. In fact, in your chosen profession it's important to rise above the mediocrity of most people and decide to be yourself, brilliantly. In fact, we're going to be blunt here: it's your job to be positive, and if you think you can't be you need to find a different job. Children need positive people to help them succeed.

Of course, we all have bad days. We all have a background story in our personal lives which at times makes it hard to wear that smile of happiness with conviction, but remember those cabin staff as we boarded our aircraft. Who knows if any of them were having a difficult time in their personal lives? Who knows if one of them was not feeling 100% on that particular day? But once they were in uniform and performing on their professional stage, they created the weather. It was a deliberate choice to do so. It was exactly the same when Chris bumped into Bob in a well-known supermarket as he stacked his weekly shopping onto the conveyor belt. After fighting his way around the store, fending off folks trying to flog him car insurance and a taste of the new oriental cooking sauce, and locating his trolley after someone had moved it to the next isle clearly thinking it was theirs, Chris was not bursting with bonhomie. Bob (he had a nametag) was the guy on the till who banished Chris's downbeat mood. Bob sang, chuckled and jollied his way through the piled up shopping as it trundled towards the barcode reader. Chris, partly bemused, passed the time of day, to which Bob responded, 'I'm living the dream!'

the Smile of happiness

Wear it with conviction!

Living the dream? Top answer from Bob, eh? Now, we don't think Bob was suggesting that the whole of his life had been planned out by him to reach this particular pinnacle on a supermarket till, but what is clear is that Bob had chosen to be happy and by choosing he was making others happy too. It's worth noting that your happiness is a mix of your genes, circumstances and choices in about a 50/10/40 mix. That means that your choice of attitude counts far more than your working environment. Back to Bob for a second: working on a checkout in a supermarket was accounting for 10% of his happiness but his positive attitude was weighing in with a whopping 40%. So, exactly like Bob, we can decide how to be in our professional role and we can decide how to feel. And if we get it right, other people will catch our positivity too.

Here it is with no punches pulled: the impact you are having on those around you is profound. You are not in a factory or on a checkout – you are a classroom assistant. You are in the people business. And not just any old people, *young people*, specially selected because they desperately need a leg up. So we're not talking about messing about on the edges of their lives; we're talking about a whopping and potentially life-changing positive impact on the life chances of young people. Fact.

Andy has been studying what he calls 'flourishing' for the best part of ten years, and flourishing is when your emotions positively impact on those around you. He calls them '2%ers' – the people you can count on the fingers of one hand who inspire you when they walk into a room. There is something special about them, usually something as simple as a smile, an energy or a warmth. In corporate terms you can measure their impact in terms of increased sales or productivity. That is not so easy in our game, but you can still spot a 2%er when you see one. They are people who are an absolute pleasure to work with, and being an absolute pleasure to work with should be the aim of every classroom assistant. The person you can always go to and they will always respond. The person who will take the initiative and sort out whatever needs sorting. The person you really miss if they have to take time off. The person who cheers everyone up on a Monday morning. The person who lights up the room when they enter. For the sake of the staff and children, we urge you to put a bit of energy into your thinking and be the staffroom 2%er.

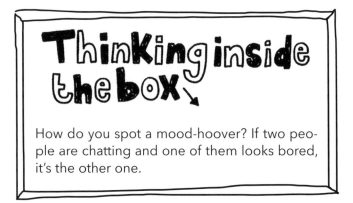

How do you spot a mood-hoover? If two people are chatting and one of them looks bored, it's the other one.

Not only are the very best classroom assistants 2%ers themselves but they know how to deal with mood-hoovers. It can be very hard if you work alongside a teacher, caretaker, curriculum leader or even, dare we say it, head teacher who is habitually negative and always wanting to see the worst in everything.

Most of us who work in education will meet children who are mood-hoovers too: the ones who announce their arrival at the beginning of the class with the catch-all phrase used by all disaffected kids, 'This is *boooring*.' Brilliant classroom assistants disarm these youngsters by distracting them into territory they are engaged via mini-conversations, and then weave a tapestry of strategies which bring them back round to engaging with the learning. Brilliant classroom

assistants bounce around negative colleagues without being dragged down into their trough of despair.

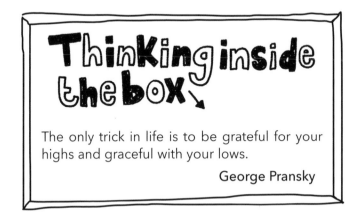

The only trick in life is to be grateful for your highs and graceful with your lows.

George Pransky

Gary once had a member of staff who was a typical mood-hoover and when he told her so she came back at him with, 'So you actually want me to pretend to be happy?' A lost cause as it turned out, as the only way that member of staff was going to be happy was if there was no possibility of anything being good. This person was in a downward spiral of negativity and it led to the end of what could have been a great career. Once fixed in this black hole of despair there was no escape – or no desire for it anyway.

For our 2%ers, however, there is always escape. Don't think for one minute that we believe you can be positive about everything in every moment of your breathing day. You're a human being so you will have your share of life's challenges and things that naturally make you sad. As Robert Holden observes, anyone who has reached the ripe old age of 30 has enough reasons to be miserable for the rest of their life. The difference is that by choosing the sunny side of life you will bounce back from mistakes, sadness and setbacks. In fact, if you're a bona fide 2%er you might even 'bounce forward', meaning that you will learn from your mistakes and come back a stronger and better person.

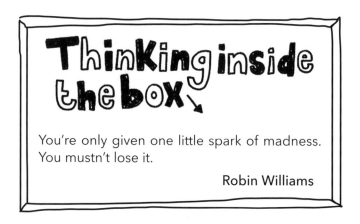

Thinking inside the box

You're only given one little spark of madness. You mustn't lose it.

Robin Williams

So it's your choice then. We recommend it. Not just because if you go for it you'll get up every morning reminding yourself that the world is actually a fab place and you're looking forward to another great day with some awesome kids, but because that choice will change your life beyond work. Your positivity will get you noticed, and being noticed will most likely bring you promotion or a pay rise. It is also likely to bring you better health and, best of all, a longer life. Now, is that a deal to turn down? It only needs your commitment to be your best self.

Being a 2%er will bring you...

- Better health ♥
- A promotion £££
- A longer life ☺

How will you know whether you're a 2%er? Well, first, your colleagues will tell you that you're brilliant to have on board. You will take part on equal terms with the teaching staff in everything the school offers, volunteering for trips, helping with the make-up for the shows and dressing up

on Red Nose Day or for Children in Need. You will be on the front line when the chips are down. You will notice when the teacher is off colour with a winter cold and offer to put the kettle on (while the mood-hoovers remain self-centred and oblivious, having ensconced themselves in a comfy chair in their corner of the staffroom). You will be in the dinner hall when it's raining cats and dogs at lunchtime and hundreds of kids have descended on the dinner queue like the feeding of the 5,000. You will be everywhere but, most importantly, you will be beaming and loving every minute of it!

TOP TIPS

- Avoid negative colleagues. Or, if you can't avoid them, take them on as a challenge and ask yourself, 'What is this person teaching me today?' (The likely answer is to remain tolerant and upbeat even when presented with negativity.)

- Choose to be positive. It's worth 40% of your total happiness and it's totally down to you.

- Take personal responsibility for being your best self. Yes, there is effort involved in rising above mediocrity but the effort pays back a million times over.

- It's okay to have an occasional off day but learn to bounce back. Today is a new day and a fresh start.

FINAL BELL

Thinking inside the box

No one can go back and make a brand new start, but anyone can start from now and make a brand new ending.

Anon.

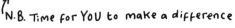

N.B. Time for YOU to make a difference

So we come to the end of our journey. We hope you have enjoyed travelling with us and we

hope that you will want to continue to build your career as a brilliant classroom assistant, because if you do you will make a difference to lots of kids' lives and they will thank you for it.

It is not a cliché to say that no two days are ever the same in education and the variety is infinite. You will enjoy highs and lows along the way, and we hope you will burn with that passion which accompanies wanting to improve and better yourself on a daily basis.

As we take our leave of you, we wish you wind in your sails as you venture to the yonder horizons of personal achievement. Brilliant classroom assistants are true professionals and they make a difference.

You can't opt out of having a mission. Whether you know or acknowledge it, you're living the mission you've chosen. Even the basic existence of eating, sleeping and slouching in front of the TV is a mission, of sorts – a mission of sloth and ease. The key is to choose your calling dynamically rather than acting it out passively which, in essence, is what this book is all about.

Life is the sum of all your choices.

attributed to Albert Camus

Perspective is everything. On one level we are a tiny pinprick of life on a speck of solar dust, drifting among billions of other specks. We have 28,000 days, a terrifyingly insignificant fraction of the universe's 14 billion years. This can make you feel so insignificant that, what's the point? In the grand scheme of the entirety of the universe our existence represents less than the blink of an eye. But if we zoom in the perspective can be hugely liberating. It can release you from the shackles of self-importance. Why not go for it (whatever 'it' ends up being)? As Ruby Wax suggests, maybe we need to trust life and ourselves a bit more and see how things unfold, rather than trying to grab the wheel the whole time.

Let's just remind you of your default setting from earlier – remember, the Ready Brek glow? We suggested that when you were a kid you would turn everything into an adventure and a humble cardboard box would become a rocket or pirate ship. You were born excited, curious and positive, but somewhere along the way most people just kind of forget.

So when you look at an empty cardboard box, what do you see now? Is it just a boring box made out of brown cardboard? Or is it a wizard's castle, a grand prix racing car, a TARDIS or a pirate ship? Next time you sit down opposite Chelsea, Chad or Chloe, what will you see? Will you see a child who finds engaging in learning difficult, or a sparkling opportunity for you to help create something wondrous?

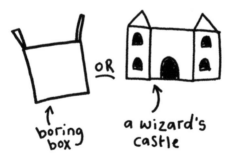

OR

boring box

a wizard's castle

And if we stretch the analogy to your life, what do you feel? Is life a bit humdrum and flat? Or could you inject some childlike excitement and see it as a daring adventure?

Let's pose two questions and a challenge for the pirate within:

1   If you had a 'reset' button would you want to press it?

2   More to the point, would you be brave enough to press it?

Our challenge? *We dare you!*

EDUCATIONAL TERMS, ABBREVIATIONS AND ACRONYMS

The world of education loves creating unfathomable terms for all sorts of things, and then, just when you think you've grasped them, they change again or more are added to the list. This little collection is to help you see through the foggy layers of jargon you'll come across. You'll never know it all and this doesn't even scratch the surface but it's a helping hand. (Oh, apart from the spoof one we've thrown in to keep you on your toes!)

A level Advanced level

Achievement The progress made by a pupil

Added value The progress pupils make

ADHD Attention deficit hyperactivity disorder

ASD Autism spectrum disorder

Attainment The standard a pupil has reached – for example, in an assessment

AWPU Age weighted pupil unit – used in allocating school finances

Banding Portions of students organised on the timetable by ability

Base line The starting point from which to measure progress

BSP Behaviour support plan

BTEC Business and Technology Education Council

CAT Cognitive ability test

CPD Continuing professional development

DBS Disclosure and Barring Service

DfE Department for Education (changes frequently though)

DT Design and technology (sometimes includes A for art)

EAL English as an additional language

EDS Excessive daytime sleepiness (you may find this in period 5)

EFL English as a foreign language

EHCP Education, health and care plan

EIP Education Improvement Partnership

EP Educational psychologist

FFT Fischer Family Trust – a group that analyses performance data

FSM Free school meals

G&T Gifted and talented

GCSE General Certificate of Secondary Education

HLTA Higher level teaching assistant

HMI Her Majesty's Inspector

HOD Head of department

HOF Head of faculty

HOY Head of year (or year head)

IEP Individual education plan

IIP Investors in People

Improvement plan A timed targeted plan with success criteria to deal with weaknesses

ITT Initial teacher training

JPD Joint professional development

KS1 Key Stage (can be 1, 2, 3, 4, 5)

LA Local authority

LAC Looked after children

LSA Learning support assistant

MFL Modern foreign languages

MLD Moderate learning disability

NEET Not in education, employment or training

NoR Number on roll

NPQH National Professional Qualification for Headship

NQT Newly qualified teacher

Ofsted Office for Standards in Education

P1 Period 1 (e.g. on the timetable)

PAN Planned admission number

PE Physical education

Performance tables Published league tables of schools' results data

PM Performance management

PP Pupil premium

PRU Pupil referral unit

PTA Parent-teacher association

Safeguarding Child protection procedures in schools

SAT Standard assessment task

SEND Special educational needs and disability

Setting Grouping classes by ability

SS Social services

TA Teaching assistant

UCAS University and Colleges Admissions Service

VAK Visual, auditory and kinaesthetic

Yr 1 Year (can be 1-13)

BIBLIOGRAPHY

BBC News (2013). Cosmetic Injections Depression Link, (11 April). Available at: http://www.bbc.co.uk/news/health-22106569.

Brazelton, T. Berry (1992). *Heart Start: The Emotional Foundations of School Readiness* (Arlington, VA: National Center for Clinical Infant Programs).

Carnegie, Dale (1936). *How to Win Friends and Influence People* (New York: Simon & Schuster).

Children's Society (2015). *Good Childhood Report 2015* (London: Children's Society). Available at: http://www.childrenssociety.org.uk/what-we-do/resources-and-publications/the-good-childhood-report-2015.

Claxton, Guy (2002). *Building Learning Power: Helping Young People Become Better Learners* (Bristol: TLO).

Cope, Andy and Whittaker, Andy (2012). *The Art of Being Brilliant: Transform Your Life by Doing What Works for You* (Chichester: Capstone).

Dossey, Larry (1982). *Space, Time and Medicine* (Boston, MA: Shambhala Publications).

Dweck, Carol S. (2006). *Mindset: The New Psychology of Success* (New York: Random House).

Field, Frank (2011). Breaking the Cycle of Deprivation to Prevent Poor Children from Becoming Poor Adults. Keynote speech at the Raise the Aspirations and Achievement of Deprived Pupils Conference, London, 28 September.

Gallup Business Journal (1999). Item 5: My Supervisor Cares About Me (19 April). Available at: http://www.

gallup.com/businessjournal/493/item-supervisor-cares-about.aspx.

Gardner, Howard (1993). *Frames of Mind: The Theory of Multiple Intelligences* (New York: Basic Books).

Gardner, Howard (1993). *Multiple Intelligences: The Theory in Practice* (New York: Basic Books).

Ginott, Haim (1971). *Teacher and Child: A Book for Parents and Teachers* (New York: Macmillan).

Goleman, Daniel (2007). *Social Intelligence: The New Science of Human Relationships* (London: Arrow).

Guardian, The (2015). Online all the time – average British household owns 7.4 internet devices (9 April). Available at: http://www.theguardian.com/technology/2015/apr/09/online-all-the-time-average-british-household-owns-74-internet-devices.

Hart, Betty and Risley, Todd R. (2003). The Early Catastrophe: The 30 Million Word Gap by Age 3, *American Educator* (Spring): 4–9.

Langer, Ellen J. (2005). *On Becoming an Artist: Reinventing Yourself Through Mindful Creativity* (New York: Random House).

Lewinsohn, Peter M., Rohde, Paul, Seeley, John R. and Fischer, Scott A. (1993). Age Cohort Changes in the Lifetime Occurrence of Depression and Other Mental Disorders, *Journal of Abnormal Psychology* 102 (1993): 110–120.

Meaney, Michael J. (2001). Maternal Care, Gene Expression, and the Transmission of Individual Differences in Stress Reactivity Across Generations, *Annual Review of Neuroscience* 24: 1161–1192.

Munby, Steve (2014). Learning Centred Leadership. Keynote speech delivered at the Inspiring Leadership Conference, June. Available at: http://cdn.cfbt.com/~/

media/CfBTCorporate/Files/Resources/
inspiring-leadership-2014/keynote-Steve-Munby-
Inspiring-Leadership-Speech.pdf.

Pierson, Rita (2013) Every Kid Needs a Champion, *TED.
com* (May). Available at: https://www.ted.com/talks/
rita_pierson_every_kid_needs_a_
champion?language=en.

Pinker, Steven (1997). *How the Mind Works* (New York:
W.W. Norton).

Powdthavee, Nattavudh (2008). Putting a Price Tag on
Friendships, Relatives, and Neighbours: Using Surveys
of Life Satisfaction to Value Social Relationships, The
Journal of Socio-economics 37(4): 1459–1480.
Available at: http://www.powdthavee.co.uk/resources/
valuing_social_relationships_15.04.pdf.

Robinson, Ken (2010). Bring On the Learning
Revolution! *TED.com* (May). Transcript available at:
https://www.ted.com/talks/sir_ken_robinson_bring_
on_the_revolution/transcript?language=en.

Sharma, Robin (2011). Powerful Tactics to Lead Without
a Title (30 August). Available at: http://www.
robinsharma.com/blog/tag/lead-without-a-title/.

Stern, Daniel N. (2004). *The Present Moment in
Psychotherapy and Everyday Life* (New York: W.W.
Norton).

Sutton Trust and Education Endowment Foundation
(2014). *Sutton Trust-EEF Teaching and Learning Toolkit.*
Available at: https://educationendowmentfoundation.
org.uk/uploads/toolkit/EEF_Teaching_and_learning_
toolkit_Feb_2014.pdf.

Syed, Matthew (2011). *Bounce: The Myth of Talent and
the Power of Practice* (London: Fourth Estate).

Taylor, David (2007). *The Naked Coach: Business
Coaching Made Simple* (Chichester: Capstone).

Weissman, Myrna M., Wickramaratne, Priya, Greenwald, Steven et al. (1992). The Changing Rate of Major Depression: Cross-National Comparisons, *Journal of the American Medical Association* 268 (21): 3098–3105.

ABOUT THE AUTHORS

Chris and Gary come from completely different backgrounds but both have developed a similar passion for teaching, and between them they have over seventy years' experience in the classroom. Both fizz with energy and crackle with creative ideas for engaging kids.

Chris trained as a French teacher in London secondary schools before taking up his first post in an 11-18 comprehensive in Tamworth, and then moving on to Leicestershire. He moved to a middle school to take on more responsibility as a head of modern foreign languages, eventually becoming deputy head of an 11-16 academy. Between those last two posts, the true luvvie in Chris came to the fore and he led the school's specialist status as an arts college, a key aspect of the school gaining an Ofsted grade of outstanding. This also involved teaching in partner primary schools. Unsurprisingly, he has turned his hand very successfully to teaching drama too and has written and directed school productions with casts of up to 170 students.

Gary started in the north of England and yo-yoed around the country from Milton Keynes to Norwich, to Sunderland and back down to Leicestershire. He is a design technologist by trade but eighteen years ago, after plugging various gaps in science and humanities, he became a permanent fixture in the English department, teaching at top primary and secondary level. He continued to teach English as a head teacher. He was head of the same secondary school for fifteen years but

also led two others, the latter being a pupil referral unit which he (alongside colleagues) took out of special measures.

Chris and Gary are highly experienced teachers with success both in the classroom and in leading teaching and learning. Their company, Decisive Element, is one of the country's most popular for workshops, keynote speeches and inspiration.

Outside of education, Chris is a keen cricketer, walker and amateur thespian, while Gary plays football, skis and climbs mountains.

Andy describes himself as a qualified teacher, author and learning junkie. He has spent most of his adult life exploring the science of positive psychology, happiness and flourishing, culminating in a PhD from the University of Loughborough. Andy delivers his flagship Art of Being Brilliant workshops and keynotes all over the world, and is fortunate enough to count DHL, Toyota, Microsoft, IKEA and Hewlett Packard among his customers. Andy also delivers workshops for children and teachers (basically, to anyone who will listen!). He has written a series of self-help and personal development books around the themes of happiness and well-being. Bizarrely, Andy also leads a double life as a children's author. He has penned the bestselling Spy Dog series for Puffin and is a co-author of *The Art of Being a Brilliant Teenager* (Capstone, 2014). He lives in Derbyshire with his wife, teenagers and pet pigs.

Andy's website is www.artofbrilliance.co.uk and he can be contacted at andy@artofbrilliance.co.uk, or you can follow his very happy tweets at @beingbrilliant.

Published by
Crown House Publishing
Crown Buildings, Bancyfelin, Carmarthen, Wales, SA33 5ND, UK
www.crownhouse.co.uk
and
Crown House Publishing Company LLC
6 Trowbridge Drive, Suite 5, Bethel, CT 06801-2858, USA
www.crownhousepublishing.com

© Gary Toward, Chris Henley and Andy Cope 2016

Illustrations © Amy Bradley, 2016

First published 2016.

Edited by Andy Cope

British Library of Cataloguing-in-Publication Data
A catalogue entry for this book is available from the British Library.

Print ISBN 978-178583022-8
Mobi ISBN 978-178583057-0
ePub ISBN 978-178583058-7
ePDF ISBN 978-178583059-4

LCCN 2015953562

Printed and bound in the UK by
Gomer Press, Llandysul, Ceredigion

W9-BJG-758

THE ART OF BEING A
BRILLIANT
CLASSROOM
ASSISTANT

GARY TOWARD, CHRIS HENLEY
AND ANDY COPE

Crown House Publishing Limited
www.crownhouse.co.uk